Inca

Mytl

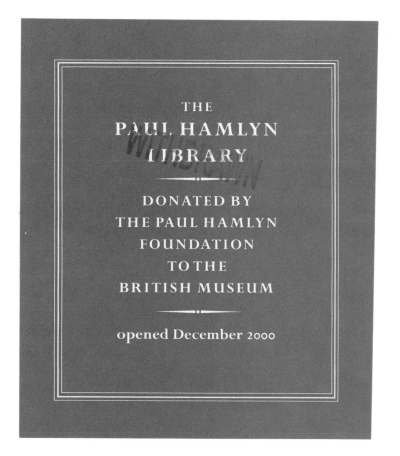

For My Mother, Bernice Coslett

Acknowledgements

I would like to express my great appreciation to Frank Salomon, Julia Meyerson, Tony Aveni, Colin McEwan and Nicole Casi, who read and commented on earlier drafts of this work. I alone am responsible for any errors that remain. Colin McEwan was both generous and accommodating in facilitating my work in the British Museum and in the photo archives of the Museum of Mankind. I also thank Clara Bezanilla, who provided invaluable assistance in the British Museum collections. Thanks to Christopher Donnan and Michael Moseley for granting permission to reproduce illustrations. Finally, at British Museum Press, I thank Nina Shandloff, who was both gracious and persistent in getting this project underway, and Coralie Hepburn, who guided the work to its final conclusion with utmost efficiency and congeniality.

Inca

Myths

GARY URTON

Published for The Trustees of The British Museum by BRITISH MUSEUM PRESS

First published in 1999 by British Museum Press
A division of The British Museum Company Ltd
46 Bloomsbury Street, London WC1B 3QQ

A catalogue record for this book is available from
the British Library

ISBN 0 7141 1791 9

Designed by Martin Richards
Cover design by Slatter-Anderson
Maps by John Gilkes
Set in 10 ½ pt Sabon and printed in Great Britain
by The Bath Press, Avon

This page: Lake Titicaca.

Front cover: Inca miniature llama figurine,
made of gold.

Contents

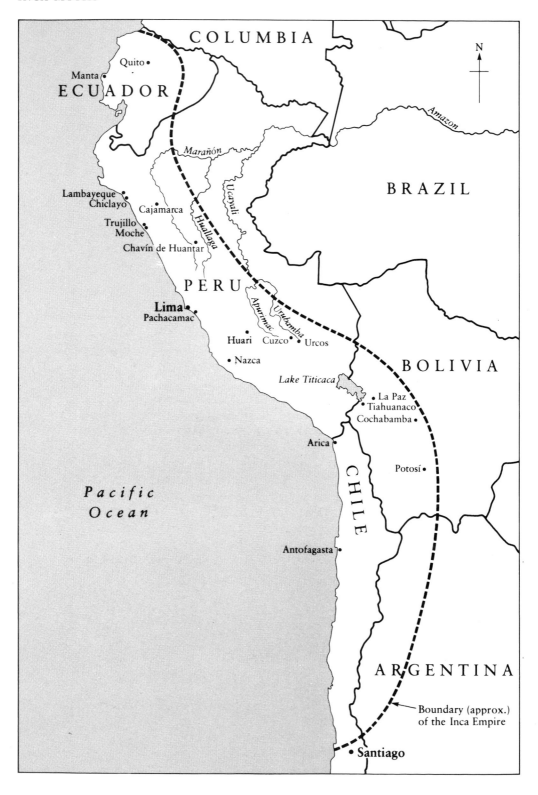

N

COLUMBIA

ECUADOR

Quito •

Manta •

BRAZIL

Amazon

Marañón

Ucayali

Lambayeque •
Chiclayo •
Cajamarca •

Trujillo •
Moche •

Chavín de Huantar •

Huallaga

PERU

Lima •
Pachacamac •

Apurimac

Urubamba

Huari •   Cuzco • • Urcos

• Nazca

Lake Titicaca

BOLIVIA

• La Paz
• Tiahuanaco
Cochabamba •

Arica •

• Potosí

Pacific
Ocean

CHILE

Antofagasta •

ARGENTINA

Boundary (approx.)
of the Inca Empire

• Santiago

Introduction:
the settings of Inca myths in
space and time

The land and people of Tahuantinsuyu

The Andes, home of the Incas, are made up of three parallel chains of mountains in western South America which run like a colossal nerve fibre from north-west to south-east, through the centre of the modern nation-states of Ecuador, Peru and Bolivia (see map). The northern boundary of the empire lay near the present-day border between Ecuador and Colombia, while its southern reaches extended nearly halfway down the length of what is now Chile and eastwards into north-western Argentina. The Incas divided this territory into four parts, and they knew this land, and their empire, by the name *Tahuantinsuyu*, 'the four united quarters'.

Although the Inca empire is commonly referred to as an 'Andean civilization', a phrase evoking the image of a society adapted to a rugged, essentially mountainous terrain, this view in fact obscures the great environmental complexity and ecological diversity that existed within the territory controlled by this ancient society. For while the rugged terrain of the Andes mountains did indeed make up the core of Inca territory, it was the relationship between the highlands and two adjacent strips of lowlands which gave Inca civilization its true environmental richness and cultural complexity.

One of these lowland strips is an exceptionally dry coastal desert lying along the western edge of the continental shelf, washed by the frigid waters of the Humboldt Current. Numerous rivers emerge from the foothills of the Andes to flow westward to the Pacific Ocean across this dry coastal plain, forming fertile ribbon-like oases which were the home sites of numerous pre-Columbian civilizations. The other lowland region, stretching along the eastern edge of the Andes, includes the humid tropical forest watersheds of the Amazon and Paraná river basins.

Within Peru, the core of Inca territory, several large intermontane tributaries of the Amazon, such as the Marañón, Huallaga and Ucayali rivers, start out by flowing northwards but then break out of the mountains toward the east, running down through rugged foothills into the tropical forest lowlands. These riverine arteries, connecting the upper Amazon with the eastern Andean foothills, have served for millennia as important routes of travel and communication linking the human populations of these two vast ecological regions.

The environmental setting in which Inca civilization thrived thus incorporated the three major ecological zones of coast, mountains and tropical forest, each of which was home to a seeming myriad local and regional ethnic groups. Through years of archaeological research and the study of early colonial documents, researchers have arrived at a widely shared understanding of how the Incas and their neighbours adapted their social, economic, political and ritual institutions to the land of Tahuantinsuyu. In some cases, this involved reliance on tried-and-true practices inherited from earlier civilizations; in other cases, the Incas were challenged to devise new institutions, adaptive strategies, and principles and practices of rulership. In the broadest terms, we should give special emphasis to one institution in particular and describe its relationship to a widespread strategy of adaptation by means of which at least late pre-Hispanic Andean societies met the challenges of adapting to this particular environmental setting. The institution in question was the *ayllu*, and the strategy was the exploitation of resources in multiple ecological zones.

Ayllus – a Quechua word meaning 'family', 'lineage' or 'part' – of which there were perhaps several tens of thousands spread throughout that part of the Andes incorporated within the Inca empire, were kinship, landholding and ritual-ceremonial groupings. The membership of each ayllu was distributed discontinuously over a wide area. That is, some members of the ayllu would live at a mid-altitudinal setting; others would inhabit the high *puna* (tundra) zone; and still others would occupy settlements in lower-lying areas, including the intermontane valleys and the coastal and/or tropical forest lowlands. The economy of each ayllu was based on the exchange of goods among members who lived in different ecological zones. Such exchanges may have gone on both through the relatively continuous movement of individuals belonging to the group as they travelled (probably in llama caravans) between ayllu settlements, as well as during annual gatherings, or festivals, of ayllu members held at some central settlement. We know that the ayllus maintained ancestral mummies, which were venerated by the group as a whole. Ayllu festivals would have provided the setting both for the veneration of these ancestral mummies, and for the retelling of the origin myths of the ayllus.

In addition to ayllus, researchers often speak of the presence of different 'ethnic groups' in the Inca empire. In the Inca case, this nomenclature refers to groupings of ayllus that recognized a higher-level unity among themselves, often tracing their common origins back to the ancestor(s) of the ancestors of the various ayllus. Such collectivities of ayllus also constituted what are referred to (particularly in the southern Andes) as confederations. Another common, intermediate-level of organization throughout the empire were two-part – so-called 'moiety' – groupings of ayllus. In many cases, the two

Group of Inca polished stone mortars in the shape of llamas.

parts, which were commonly referred to as 'upper' (*hanan*) and 'lower' (*hurin*), derived from a locally important topographic and hydrological division, recognized most clearly in the distribution of water through a network of irrigation canals. In addition, the ancestors of the moieties were often thought to have had different origins and/or specializations (e.g., farmers/herders, or autochthonous peoples/invaders).

The genius of Inca civilization was its successful integration of these many and varied peoples and resources into a single, hierarchically organized society. This was achieved by processes of conquest and alliance, as well as by a high level of bureaucratic organization, which allowed the state not only to co-ordinate and direct the activities of these numerous ayllus, ethnic groups and confederations, but also to integrate and synthesize what I will term below the 'mythic-histories' of these various groups. In this regard, it will be useful to establish from the beginning two important, interrelated distinctions that should be made concerning religious and mythic traditions in the pre-Columbian Andes. One distinction is that between Andean religion and Inca religion, while the other is that between Andean myths and Inca myths.

As it is generally understood by specialists working in the Andes, 'Andean religion' refers to locally based sets of beliefs and practices that identify and pay homage to local earth, mountain, and water spirits and to the deities that were linked to local (i.e., provincial) ayllus and ethnic groups and their ancestors throughout the empire. These beliefs and practices were linked to, and explicated by, cosmic origin myths, myths of primordial relations between humans and animals, and accounts of mythical encounters between the ancestors of different ayllus and ethnic groups within a given area that were retained by the story-tellers within that region.

'Inca religion', on the other hand, encompasses the beliefs, ceremonies and ritual practices that were promoted by the Inca nobility and their priestly and political agents for the benefit of the Inca state. Inca mythology refers to the mythological traditions that contextualized, explained and justified state beliefs and practices to the subjects of the Incas. Although there were numerous similarities and interconnections between the two, the focus of Andean religion and mythology was on the unity and perpetuation of each of the myriad ayllus and ethnic groups, whereas the driving force behind Inca religion and mythology was the unification of all such local groups within the empire in the service, and under the hegemony, of the Incas.

Central to the practice of Inca and Andean religion was the worship of and care for mummies. Reverence for and continuous care of the mummies of the Inca kings, as well as the ancestral mummies, called *mallquis*, of ayllus were important practices in the religion of people throughout the Inca empire. Numerous myths were told by the Incas and their provincial subjects concerning the life and deeds of those individuals whose mummified remains were prominently displayed in public places, or were stored in caves near the towns where their descendants lived. It was believed that caring for, redressing, and offering food and drink to the ancestral mummies were requirements for maintaining cosmic order, as well as the continued fertility of the crops and herd animals. Such beliefs and practices continued to haunt the Spanish priests who struggled for centuries to stamp out such 'idolatrous' practices and to Christianize the descendants of the Incas and their provincial subjects.

The organization of the Inca empire

At the centre of the empire was the capital city, Cusco, located in a fertile valley in the south-central Andes of Peru at an altitude of about 3,400 m (11,000 ft) above sea level. Cusco was home to the royal lineage of the Incas, from which was drawn the dozen kings who ruled the empire from sometime near the beginning of the 1400s until the Spanish conquest of the Andes in 1532. The population of the city, and by extension the empire as a whole, was divided into four ritual and administrative districts, called *suyus* ('part', 'quarter'). Beginning in the north-west and going clockwise, the four quarters were called Chinchaysuyu, Antisuyu, Collasuyu and Cuntisuyu. The quarters were produced by a complicated intersection of two dual divisions within the city of Cusco. The true centre of the city of Cusco and of the four quarters of the city and the empire was the set of a half-dozen or so buildings called the Coricancha ('golden enclosure'), which is sometimes referred to as the Temple of the Sun.

One room of the Coricancha housed the mummies of past kings of the empire. These were taken out of the Coricancha during important ritual celebrations and, riding on litters, were paraded around the central plaza of the city. In other rooms of the Coricancha were images and idols depicting and dedicated to the creator deity (Viracocha), the Sun, the Moon, Venus (of

The four quarters of the Inca empire.

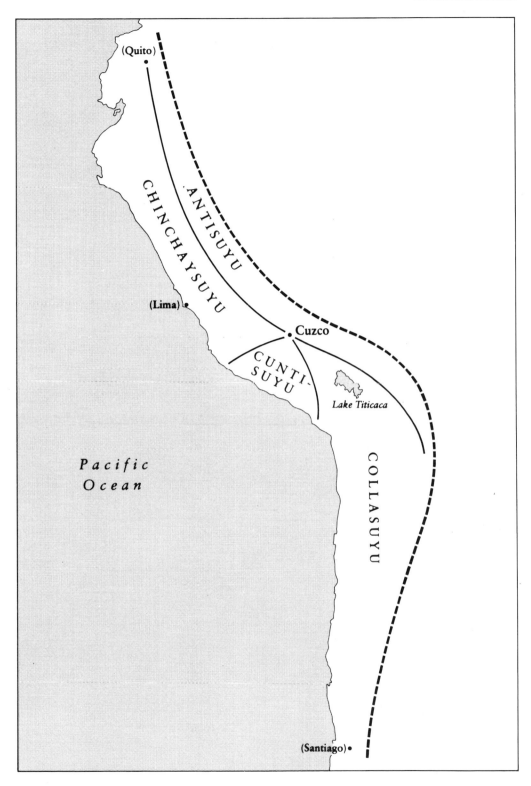

(Quito)

ANTISUYU

CHINCHAYSUYU

(Lima)

Cuzco

CUNTI-
SUYU

Lake Titicaca

Pacific
Ocean

COLLASUYU

(Santiago)

Eastern rooms of the Coricancha in Cusco.

the Morning and Evening), Thunder, the Rainbow, and other lesser objects of worship. While the Coricancha was the focal point of ritual life within the capital, the palaces, shrines and population of Cusco represented the focal point of the empire of Tahuantinsuyu as a whole.

At the top of the imperial hierarchy stood the Inca king, called *sapa* ('unique', 'sole') *Inca*. The ruling Inca was believed to be the direct descendant of the first king, Manco Capac, as well as the earthly manifestation of the sun (*inti*), whose light and warmth made the world of the high Andes habitable. Alongside the king was his primary wife, called the *qoya* ('queen'), who was, at least in late imperial times, also his sister. The queen was considered to be the human embodiment of the moon (*quilla*), the celestial body whose monthly rhythm of waxing and waning established the tempo of ritual life in the capital. Around the Inca king and queen were the nobility – the descendants of the dozen or so royal ayllus, or kin groups (called *panacas*), that occupied the capital. The panaca groupings were ranked hierarchically depending on their closeness to the line(s) of kings descended from Manco Capac.

In addition to his primary wife, the king had numerous secondary wives – different Spanish sources say between forty and a hundred. These women were often the daughters of high-ranking provincial aristocrats whose marriage to the Inca elevated the rank of their natal lineage and ayllu. Children of secondary wives were considered to be lower-ranking nobles, and many became administrative officials of the empire. They were supplemented by accountants, record-keepers, diviners, military commanders and other functionaries who belonged to lineages of panacas or ayllus composing the lesser nobility.

From the capital, administrators went out to the four quarters of the empire to oversee and regulate affairs of state, especially to oversee the performance of state labour. In the Inca empire 'tribute' was assessed in the form of public labour, the local ayllus having the obligation to work the lands, or herd the flocks of camelids, of the king and the gods in their local communities, as well as to perform 'turns of service' (*mit'a*) at state installations. For such purposes, the tribute-payers were organized into decimal groupings (i.e., groupings of 5, 10, 100, 500, 1000, etc. households). The state administration was similarly organized in a decimal fashion, with overseers designated to direct the affairs of different levels of decimal household groupings, keeping records on a device, called a *quipu* ('knot', see p.26), that recorded the information in a decimal-based numeration. Imperial runners (*chaskis*) carried messages between the capital and its provincial administrative centres, located at ecologically and demographically critical nodal points throughout the empire.

Numerous rituals and state ceremonies, such as the daily sacrifice of a hundred llamas in the plaza in Cusco and the celebration of two great festivals of the sun at the times of the solstices in December and June, as well as a festival of the moon in October, sanctified the unity and antiquity of collective life under the stewardship of the Incas.

In the provinces, the majority of the population was made up of commoners, or *hatunruna* ('the great people'), who were organized into a multitude of ayllus. Among the settlements occupying any given region, the highest-ranking lineage(s) among those groups held hereditary lordships, called *curacas*. The curacas acted as local authorities and imperial agents, overseeing affairs of state on behalf of the Incas within their home territories.

One particularly dramatic ceremonial expression of the unity between the Inca in the capital and the people in the countryside was the annual sacrifice of specially designated victims (usually children) called *capacochas*. These individuals were sent from the provinces to Cusco where they were sanctified by the priests of the Incas. The capacochas were then returned to their home territories, marching in sacred procession along straight lines (*ceques*), where they were sacrificed. We learn from colonial documents of capacochas being buried alive in specially constructed shaft-tombs, and recently there have been discoveries of capacochas sacrificed by being clubbed and their bodies left on high mountain tops. In all such cases, the sacrifices sealed bonds of alliance between the home community and the Inca in Cusco. The sacrifice of the capacochas also served to reaffirm the hierarchical relation between the Incas at the centre and high-ranking lineages in the provinces.

The Incas also employed a strategy of population control and economic organization whereby certain ayllus, or segments of them, were moved from their home territories, at the will of the Inca, for purposes such as working on state projects or serving as guards at frontier outposts. These transplanted people were called *mitimaes*. Such movements and the consequent mixing of people in imperial times undoubtedly had a profound impact on notions of origin places and (mythical) histories retained by ethnic groups throughout the empire. Finally, there was a hereditary class of servants known as *yanaconas* ('dark/servant people'). These were retainers of the royalty – people who lived on and worked the lands of the kings and the high nobility.

Like the myths of other ancient civilizations around the world, the cosmic creation myths and the origin myths of the Incas legitimized their rule and validated the hierarchical social, political and economic relations organizing society as a whole. It is important to stress, however, that the Incas drew on a store of knowledge, beliefs and practices that came down to them from earlier civilizations. This is not unusual, as few if any states of the ancient world arose entirely independently of earlier kingdom or chiefdom-level societies.

The archaeological remains of Inca and pre-Inca civilizations from Ecuador southward through Peru, Bolivia and Chile are extensive and extremely varied. For many of these cultures, we possess numerous examples of works of art displaying rich and complex iconographic representations of humans, animals, and human–animal composites that appear to represent supernatural entities. Such images and scenes as those of important person-ages standing serenely among subordinates, winged figures, and anthropo-morphized animals, plants and aquatic creatures that we see painted on ceramics, woven into textiles or hammered from lumps of gold offer modest clues as to the nature of and relations among indigenous deities, spirits and other mythological beings before the time of the Incas. Thus, exercising appropriate caution, we can contextualize, enrich and enlighten our understanding of Inca mythology by surveying the archaeological and iconographic records from pre-Inca civilizations.

Precursors to the Incas

The Incas were not the first Andean civilization to unify the peoples of western South America. In fact, it is evident to archaeologists that the Incas were able to affect unification as rapidly as they did (over a few centuries) by building on pre-existing relations, institutions of state, and habits of empire inherited from earlier peoples. Archaeologists divide Peruvian prehistory into five major periods, primarily on the basis of continuities and changes in ceramic shapes and styles over time and across space. Three of these periods are known as 'horizons', a term that is meant to indicate that these were periods of relative unity in art, architecture, ritualism and economy over broad regions in the central Andes. Intervening between the three horizons were two so-called 'intermediate' periods, which designate times and processes of local and regional (rather than pan-Andean) development.

Period	Approximate Time Range
Early Horizon	900–200 BC
Early Intermediate	200 BC–AD 500
Middle Horizon	AD 500–1000
Late Intermediate	AD 1000–1400
Late Horizon	AD 1400–1532

One of the earliest civilizations ancestral to the Incas is known as Chavín. This culture, whose extension in time and space defines the Early Horizon, takes its name from the site of Chavín de Huantar, which is situated at the point of union of two small rivers near the headwaters of the Marañon and Santa rivers, in the central Peruvian highlands. Chavín de Huantar exhibits all the trappings of Andean ceremonial centres: stone-faced pyramids with internal passageways converging on oracular chambers; open plazas situated between mounds that extend arm-like outward from the pyramids; and a complex arrangement of carved stone stelae and free-standing statuary bearing distinctive iconographic images. The themes of Chavín art are drawn from the animals, plants and aquatic life of the coast, highlands and tropical forest. Similarly, sites displaying this distinctive imagery are located from the upper Amazon westward, through the high intermontane valleys of the Andes mountains to the lush river valleys of the Pacific coastal desert.

Chavín images include animals, especially felines, in human-like poses, as well as harpy eagles, falcons and a profusion of serpents, many of which are rendered with formidable canine teeth. A common element that appears

Façade of the New Temple, Chavín de Huantar.

ubiquitously in Chavín art, and will reappear in art down to the time of the Spanish conquest, is the so-called 'staff deity'. These are standing frontal figures, perhaps representing human-animal composites or masked humans, both male and female, holding staffs or corn stalks in either hand. We do not know the precise meaning or significance of the staff deities for the Chavín peoples themselves. However, given the prominence and ubiquity with which such figures appear during Chavín times in architecture and on portable works of art in sites throughout much of present-day Peru, it is fairly certain that this character represented a supernatural force and personality of exceptional importance, perhaps a creator deity, of sorts. This conclusion is made all the more likely in view of the fact that staff deities of similar posture and with similar accoutrements appear commonly in artistic representations from Chavín until – and including – Inca times.

The Early Horizon was followed by another period of roughly equal length in which a number of regional chiefdoms allied and competed with each other for control of people and resources over the ecologically varied landscape of the Andes. It would be a mistake to think of the period following the Early Horizon, known as the Early Intermediate Period (200 BC–AD 500), as a time of chaos and cultural degeneration, despite the fact that the Incas themselves tended to portray such periods of decentralization and regionalism in precisely these terms. Instead, a number of major social, political and artistic innovations were achieved during this period.

For instance, city-building on the part of the chiefdom- or kingdom-

*Female staff deity
from Chavín-Period
painted textile.*

level societies on the north coast of Peru produced urban centres of astonishing complexity. This occurred in and around such sites as the Huaca del
Sol, in the Moche valley, and Pampa Grande, in the Lambayeque valley. The
recent discovery of the tombs of the lords of Sipan, near present-day
Chiclayo, Peru, display a level of sophistication in metallurgy matched only
by later Andean civilizations. Such works of art, rich in the imagery of feline,
jaguar–human and other animal representations, recall in certain respects
the art of Chavín. The mythology that underlay and gave meaning to
such iconography was undoubtedly shared by (or at least known to) other
contemporary civilizations of the north coast of Peru, as well as by earlier
and later Andean civilizations.

One body of artistic work from north coastal Peru that has been the
focus of a considerable amount of study and speculation by scholars interested in iconographic depictions of Andean mythological traditions is the
modelled and painted imagery of Moche ceramics. Here, particularly in
scenes painted on the bodies of stirrup-spout vessels, we see figures of
humans and anthropomorphized animals, birds and marine creatures, some
of which are thought to have been important characters in north coastal
(Moche) mythology. Several of the figures are shown in postures and
groupings that are so standardized, and are repeated with such regularity,
that scholars have suggested that the scenes depict a fairly limited number
(e.g., a couple of dozen) of widely shared mythic ritual 'themes'. The ritual
circumstances and mythological settings include such scenes as the capture

Mound constructions in the Lambayeque valley.

The Huaca del Sol, Moche valley.

Moche stirrup-spout vessel painted with images of beans and running messenger.

and sacrifice of enemy warriors, the offering of drink – which in some cases seems to represent goblets filled with the blood of sacrificial victims – by subordinates to high lords, or deities, and the passage of a character through the starry sky in a moon-shaped boat.

When we look to the south coast of Peru during the Early Intermediate Period, we find less emphasis on, or at least less evidence for, the development of large, urban centres than is evident at this same time on the north coast. Nonetheless, there were numerous ceremonial centres, such as those in the Pisco, Ica and Nazca river drainages, that probably served as regional pilgrimage centres visited by peoples belonging to different ethnic groups who gathered at these centres for a variety of ritual and economic motives. In addition, there are many cemeteries located within the south coastal Peruvian river valleys dating to the Early Horizon and Early Intermediate Period that are notable for the burial and display of mummies. Many such mummified remains are wrapped in beautifully woven and embroidered textiles displaying a wide array of both natural and supernatural iconographic images. The latter have been interpreted by researchers as having been linked to ritual practices (especially in agriculture and warfare) and mythological traditions of the valley residents.

The next era of cultural unification in the pre-Columbian Andes, a period known as the Middle Horizon (AD 500–1000), saw the emergence of two political and ritual centres. One, called Tiahuanaco, was located on the high Bolivian plateau (*altiplano*) not far inland from the south shore of Lake Titicaca; the other, called Huari, was situated in the south-central Peruvian highlands. The societies represented by these co-existing centres have been named after them.

Paracas weaving.

Gateway of the Sun, Tiahuanaco, showing central staff deity flanked by winged attendants.

While there were certainly numerous characteristics distinguishing Tiahuanaco and Huari societies, there were at the same time a number of notable similarities. Chief among the latter was a rich and complex iconography rendered in diverse media, particularly stone, cloth, ceramics and shell. Many images of religious and mythological significance appear commonly in the art of both Tiahuanaco and Huari. These include staff deities, as well as winged, running falcon-headed figures that are often shown in profile holding clubs and in some cases decapitated heads. The posture and location in architectural and other compositions of Tiahuanaco and Huari staff deities emphasize the centrality of this character in Tiahuanaco and Huari culture and attest to its probable religious, ritual and mythological continuity from similar figures in Chavín times. It is quite likely that, like the so-called creator gods of Inca times, such as Viracocha and Pachacamac, the staff deities of the Tiahuanaco and Huari peoples were considered to be responsible for the origin of humans and the fertility of crops and animals.

The staff deities and numerous free-standing, carved stone images at the site of Tiahuanaco are striking when seen *in situ* by tourists today, just as they were when viewed by travellers and pilgrims in Inca times. Inca informants in the early years following the Spanish invasion told their conquerors that the statues at Tiahuanaco represented an earlier race of giants whose origins were in an era before the appearance of the Inca kings. In fact, as we shall see, a ubiquitous theme in the mythology both of the Incas and of

Stone statue at Tiahuanaco.

their provincial subjects throughout much of present-day Peru was the claim that their ancestors came from Lake Titicaca and the site of Tiahuanaco itself.

The Late Intermediate Period (AD 1000–1400) was a second period of regional development in central Andean prehistory. This period falls between the Middle Horizon societies of Tiahuanaco and Huari and the emergence of Inca civilization, whose widespread distribution in space and time is referred to as the Late Horizon (*c.* AD 1400–1532). One society that emerged during the Late Intermediate Period and is of particular interest in terms of the study of Andean and Inca myths is that of the Chimu peoples. Chimu was a state-level society of north coastal Peru whose capital was at Chan Chan, in the Moche river valley. At Chan Chan and other sites that were incorporated into the Chimu state, we find the remains of massive, royal compounds containing open plazas, burial mounds and administrative quarters. Such sites display a variety of decorative adobe friezes, including repeated images of marine birds and sea creatures, as well as what has been interpreted as double-headed rainbow serpents.

Chimu, which is often referred to under the geographic–linguistic label *Yunga* ('lowlands'), is especially important in the study of Inca myths for two reasons: first, in the early colonial documentation we possess a number of accounts detailing relations between Chimu and Inca kings in mythic times, as well as encounters between the idols of these respective societies; second, the Chimu state represents perhaps the only other pre-Inca Andean state from which we have extant versions of origin myths. We will discuss the shape and contents of these myths later.

Adobe frieze at site of Chan Chan, Moche valley.

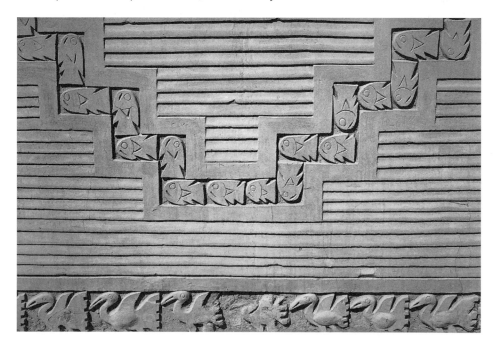

Adobe frieze depicting double-headed serpent, Huaca El Dragon, Moche valley.

The above survey provides a highly schematic overview of the succession of cultures and a periodization of the developmental phases in Andean prehistory that led up to the emergence of the Incas. Cultural developments up to the time of the Incas in the Late Horizon included kingship, a highly centralized and bureaucratic statecraft, local (ayllu-based) and state redistribution of economic resources, a priesthood, ancestor worship, and rich traditions of art and iconography in a variety of media. Although our colonial sources do not speak directly on the matter of long-term continuities of deities and mythic themes uniting one civilization and cultural phase to the next, the persistence of certain iconographic themes (e.g., feline–human hybrids, staff deities, falcon-headed warriors, or 'spirits'), and an archaeological record of the mixing and blending of cultures over time, rather than the wholesale replacement of one culture by another, lend strong support to the notion that Inca mythological traditions were the products of a long and complex process of innovation, borrowing and reworking of myths among a succession of Andean societies.

In the next chapter, we will review the early colonial sources that detail the results of these continuing Andean traditions of cosmic, state and local myths.

Sources for the study of Inca myths

How do we know about the myths the Incas told about themselves and the world around them? The first thing to note in regard to this question is that, in fact, none of what we now refer to as 'Inca myths' has come down to us from documents that were originally written by native Andean peoples in their own language(s) before the arrival of the Spaniards. This is because the Incas did not develop a system of writing – or if they did, we have not yet succeeded in identifying or deciphering it. Thus all accounts of Inca myths available to us were recorded by Spanish chroniclers or scribes, or by Spanish-trained native Andeans, all of whom wrote with pen or quill on paper or parchment. The majority of these myths were written in Spanish. However, a few early sources, such as those of the native chronicler Felipe Guaman Poma de Ayala, or of another native, Juan de Santacruz Pachacuti Yamqui Salcamaygua, are written in a Spanish liberally sprinkled with words, phrases and grammatical structures deriving either from the Inca lingua franca – a language known as Quechua – or from another widespread though unrelated language, Aymara, which was, and still is, commonly spoken around Lake Titicaca and southward, throughout much of present-day Bolivia.

At the same time as noting the absence of native written accounts of Inca myths, it is important to appreciate the role played by one indigenous recording device in particular, the *quipu*, in the collection and recording of Inca myths and histories in early colonial times. Quipus, from the Quechua word for 'knot', were linked bundles of dyed and knotted strings, which were used by the Incas to record both statistical information, such as census accounts and tribute records, as well as information that could be interpreted – in some manner that we do not yet fully understand – by experts called *quipucamayoqs* ('knot-makers or keepers') in narrating stories about the Inca past.

Before the arrival of the Spaniards, the narratives retained on the quipus were recounted by the quipucamayoqs in public settings on important ceremonial occasions. The tasks of remembering and recounting the past were also the duties of the court poet-philosophers, called *amautas*. These people were responsible for putting accounts of the genealogies and deeds of the Inca kings and queens, as well as reports of coronations, battles and so on, into song form and for performing them, on demand, before the king and the

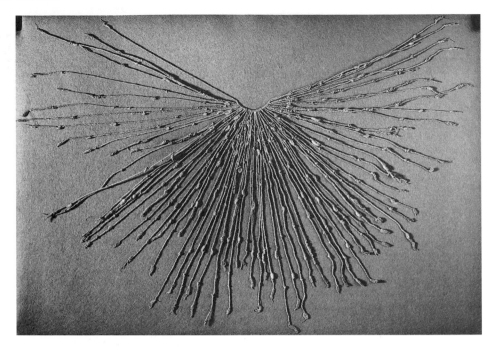

Quipu – Inca knotted-string recording device.

court. Following the Spanish conquest, these same native officials were the principal sources from whom the Spaniards heard accounts of myths, dynastic genealogies and histories, and other stories of the Inca past. In this process, the quipu accounts were 'read', or interpreted, by the quipucamayoqs in their native language, translated into Spanish by a bilingual translator (*lengua*), and written down by a Spanish scribe.

The fact that so much of the information pertaining to the Inca past collected by the Spaniards in the early years following the conquest came from (primarily male) informants in Cusco who were members of the Inca nobility gives a decidedly élitist, masculine and Cusco-centric cast to the corpus of myths available to us. It is only as we encounter documents produced during the early to mid-seventeenth century that we begin to read accounts pertaining to the lives of commoners (both women and men) in the provinces.

We must also remember that the process described above of quipu reading, translation and transcription was fraught with opportunities for both groups of people involved – natives and Spaniards – to twist, elide, embellish, or otherwise amend stories to suit their own personal or political motives. This could involve, for instance, the careful crafting of a genealogical history by a native Andean who wanted to put his or her lineage in a better light in testimony before the Spaniards. In addition, it is clear that some of the Spaniards were bent on portraying the Incas as tyrants and illegitimate rulers. This latter kind of manipulation of the past became an integral part of the Spanish strategy of justifying their own conquest of, and rule over, Andean peoples.

Qero –
colonial
drinking mug
with
Hispanicized
images of Inca
and queen.

There is, unfortunately, no magical or easy way to 'read between the lines' of mythic accounts to know what elements are indigenous and which are imposed, or imported, by natives or Europeans for some particular, political end(s). It is only by coupling a study of the colonial documents with archaeological investigations of Inca sites that we can begin to separate out myth from history in the chroniclers' accounts of Inca 'history'. Thus careful and critical study of the sources are required in order for us to arrive at what may be, in all likelihood, relevant and culturally meaningful constructions of Inca myths.

An additional point that should be borne in mind in order to appreciate fully the nature and limitations of the information on myths contained in our sources is that since the accounts available to us were all written down from informants' testimony taken after 1532, this body of myths does not possess an undisputed absolute chronology. While we can obviously follow the storyline within a given myth, noting that one event is said to have happened after another, we cannot sensibly assign an absolute date during the period before the onset of recorded history in 1532 to any one of these events solely on the basis of what the post-conquest accounts tell us.

Numerous attempts have indeed been made since the beginning of the colonial era to devise a scheme of fixed dates as a temporal framework for interpreting the possible historical significance of certain events recounted in Inca myths. These range from Spanish efforts on the one hand to correlate events mentioned in the Inca origin myths (e.g., a universal deluge, the supposed appearance of the disciples of Christ) with biblical 'history', to contemporary endeavours to impose a kind of Western, linear logic, including absolute dates, on the succession of kings said to have ruled in the Andes in late pre-Hispanic times. All such chronologies rest on shaky ground and none has been confirmed even in the most general of terms by independent, scientific archaeological investigations. It is only through the science of archaeology, with its radiocarbon and other dating techniques, that we can securely assign dates to events in the pre-Hispanic era and, thereby, begin to build up a chronological framework for evaluating the historicity of some elements of the Inca myths.

Principal chroniclers of Inca myths

The works of a couple of dozen chroniclers who wrote during the first century following the conquest provide us with material for the study of Inca mythology. Among these the following sources, discussed generally in chronological order, are some of the most interesting, useful and/or reliable.

Cieza de León was a Spanish soldier who travelled throughout much of western South America, beginning in the earliest days of Spanish penetration into the continent. Having entered Peru in about 1547, he travelled over the next several years from the far north coast, near Tumbes, southward through the former heartland of the empire and as far south as Charcas, in south-central Bolivia. Cieza was a careful observer who talked to numerous informants and took copious notes during his travels. There is much of value for the study of Inca myths in the first two parts of his *Crónica del Peru*. The first part of this work, published in 1553, contains Cieza's geographical descriptions; the second part, which carries the title *El Señorío de los Incas*, was published in 1554 and is one of our earliest sources on the history and the mythology of the Inca empire.

Juan de Betanzos was born in Spain but spent his adult life in Peru.

Around 1541, Betanzos married an Inca princess, a niece of the last undisputed king, Huayna Capac. Betanzos lived in Cusco, became fluent in the Quechua language, and was on intimate terms with numerous descendants of Inca nobility in the former capital city. In 1551 Betanzos was ordered by the Viceroy of Peru, Antonio de Mendoza, to write a history of the Incas. His account, which has recently appeared in its first English translation under the title *Narrative of the Incas* (tr. R. Hamilton and D. Buchanan, 1996), was completed in 1557. This is one of our best sources on Inca myths as told from the point of view of the Inca nobility in Cusco during the first few decades following the conquest.

Polo de Ondegardo served as the top colonial administrator (*corregidor*) of Cusco from 1558 to 1561 and again from 1571 to 1572. A jurist with a real interest in the religion, customs and 'superstitions' of the Inca peoples and their descendants, Polo carried out investigations on these and other matters – including attempts, mostly successful, to locate and dispose of the mummies of the Inca kings – during the 1550s and 1560s. These investigations resulted in the publication of a number of reports, including a treatise entitled *Los Errores y supersticiones de los indios* (1567), as well as a report on the religion and government of the Incas (1571). These provide useful background material for contextualizing our early accounts of Inca myths; material from them were digested and incorporated into a number of later works, including the chronicles by Acosta and Cobo (see below).

Polo de Ondegardo was a precursor and early proponent of a late sixteenth-century genre or tradition of interpretation and writing about the Incas and their history that developed in relation to the reorganization of the colonial state under the fourth viceroy of Peru, Francisco de Toledo (1569–81). Toledo undertook a programme of investigating Inca history, including the organization and structure of the Inca empire, as a basis for instituting reforms of virtually every aspect of life in the colony – from the operation of the colonial bureaucracy to the location and layout of native villages. Toledo also ordered the writing of several histories of the empire, based on interviews with former Inca nobility and quipucamayoqs.

The chronicles produced during or soon after the Toledan viceroyalty included such works as Sarmiento de Gamboa's *Historia de los Incas* (1572), the Cusqueñan Cristobal de Molina's *Las Fabulas y Ritos de los Incas* (1575), and José de Acosta's *Historia natural y moral de las Indias* (1590). In addition, Cabello de Balboa's *Miscelánea Antártica* (1586), an excellent source on myths of the north coast of Peru (in the area of the Chimu peoples), also incorporated materials on Inca mythology taken from the chronicle of Sarmiento de Gamboa.

A theme uniting various of these histories was the view that the Inca dynasty represented a tyrannical regime that had essentially gained power by fraudulent means. According to the Toledan interpretation, Inca rule was not only abusive, it was also illegitimate. Such assertions cleared the way for the Europeans to claim that the Spanish conquest of the Incas was a justifiable enterprise, replacing as it did the rule of a bogus nobility (that of the Incas) by the legitimate rule of the Spanish crown. Thus while the Toledan chronicles represent some of our earliest, most comprehensive and best-informed sources for the study of Inca myths, it is necessary to read them critically, with a recognition of their ideological and political underpinnings.

Another important yet somewhat problematic source on Inca mythology is the chronicle written by the *mestizo* (Spanish/Quechua mixed-blood) Garcilaso de la Vega. Garcilaso was born in Cusco in 1539, the son of an Inca princess, Isabell Chimpu Ocllo, and a Spanish *conquistador*, whose name Garcilaso bore. Garcilaso lived in Cusco until the age of twenty-one and then, in 1560, travelled to Spain, where he remained for the rest of his life. In 1602 he began writing his great history of the Inca empire, entitled *Comentarios Reales de los Incas* (1609–17). Part memoir and part compilation of earlier, especially Toledan, sources, Garcilaso's text contains numerous myths, some of which are attested to by other authors (especially Blas Valera and José de Acosta), but an equal number of which are either not found in other sources, or are indeed recounted by other authors but with notable variations from the versions remembered by Garcilaso.

At about the same time that the first part of Garcilaso's chronicle appeared, an exceptionally important text on the mythology of local peoples in the region of Huarochirí, in the central highlands of Peru, was produced. This work, which was written in the Quechua language, has been published in several languages under various titles, such as a Spanish version entitled *Dioses y Hombres de Huarochirí* and, most recently in an English translation, *The Huarochirí Manuscript* (tr. F. Salomon and G.L. Urioste, 1991). The work appears to have been composed under the direction of the local priest of this region, Francisco de Avila, although its author(s) was (were) clearly native to the area of Huarochirí. This work represents one of our best sources on the pre-Hispanic and early colonial mythological traditions of peoples in one of the former provinces of the Inca empire.

At approximately the same time that the Huarochirí manuscript was written down, a work was composed in Spain, which is known as the *Relación de los Quipucamayoqs* (1608/1542). It appears to have been assembled on behalf of a late pretender to the Inca throne, a man named Melchior Carlos Inca, in 1608. In what was an apparent attempt to add weight and legitimacy to his claims to the throne, Melchior had incorporated into the early section of his manuscript mythic materials concerning the foundation of the Inca dynasty that derived from an inquest undertaken in Cusco, in 1542, before the Licenciado Vaca de Castro. The informants at that inquest were four elderly quipucamayoqs who had served the Inca as historians before the time of the conquest. These materials represent some of the earliest origin myths of the Inca state that we have.

We should take note here of another Spanish chronicler, Antonio de la Calancha, whose *Coronica moralizada del Orden de San Augustín en el Perú* (1638) contains valuable information on the religion, customs and myths of peoples of the north coast of Peru.

An important development in the recording of myths from outside Cusco that occurred during the early seventeeth century was the appearance of chronicles written by native, Quechua-speaking authors. The most notable authors to mention in this regard are Felipe Guaman Poma de Ayala and Juan de Santacruz Pachacuti Yamqui Salcamaygua.

Guaman Poma was born in Huamanga, in the central Peruvian Andes. He claimed that his father had been a provincial nobleman who served as an emissary of the Inca Guascar to Francisco Pizarro at Cajamarca. Guaman Poma received intensive ecclesiastical training from priests in and around Huamanga, and he even participated in the 'extirpation' of native idolatries during the late sixteenth and early seventeenth centuries. In 1613 Guaman Poma completed his monumental work, entitled *Nueva Corónica y Buen Gobierno* (1583–1613). This document contains, in its approximately 1,000 pages, a description of life in Peru before, during and after the Spanish conquest. In addition to its text, the work also contains almost 400 drawings, which constitute one of our best sources of information on Inca dress, agricultural implements, and other features of everyday life, as well as depicting scenes of ritual and worship at places mentioned in some of the origin myths, such as the mountain and cave of origin of the first Inca king. While Guaman Poma was an early and ardent convert to Christianity, who believed that it was the Inca kings who had led their Andean subjects into idolatry, his chronicle contains much information of value for a study of Inca myths.

Juan de Santacruz Pachacuti Yamqui Salcamaygua was another important native author, from the area of Canas and Canchis, midway between Cusco and Lake Titicaca. Although he also wrote from the perspective of a Christian convert, he was somewhat more sympathetic to the Incas than was Guaman Poma. In his work, entitled *Relación de Antiguedades deste Reyno del Pirú* (c. 1613), Pachacuti Yamqui recounts myths, as well as a substantial body of quasi-mythic/historical data that can be linked to myths recounted by other authors. His work is decidedly idiosyncratic and challenging in its composition, given its frequent use of Quechua words and grammatical structures, yet it contains much of interest and value for the study of Inca myths.

Bernabé Cobo was a Jesuit priest who was born in Spain, entered Peru in 1599, and remained there for all but a few years of the rest of his life. Cobo travelled from Lima to Cusco in 1609, and spent much of the next twenty years undertaking missionary work and travelling in southern Peru and northern Bolivia. In 1653 he completed his great work, *Historia del Nuevo Mundo*. To date, the translator Roland Hamilton has prepared two excellent English translations of different parts of Cobo's *Historia*, under the titles, *History of the Inca Empire* (1983; books 11 and 12 of *Historia*), and *Inca Religion and Customs* (1990; books 13 and 14 of *Historia*). Cobo drew extensively on previous chronicles, including the works of Polo de Ondegardo, Cristobal de Molina, José de Acosta and Garcilaso de la Vega. He is considered by many Andeanists to be one of our most reliable sources on Inca history. Certainly the myths, descriptions of state ceremonies, and accounts of Inca religious beliefs and practices which he synthesized from earlier sources resulted in the production of our most comprehensive and balanced chronicle of life in the Inca empire.

A final set of documents that are important for the study of Inca myths are the so-called *idolatrías* ('idolatries'). These documents were produced primarily during the first half of the seventeenth century as a result of investigations by Catholic priests into what the church took to be the continuing idolatry practised by peoples in the Andean countryside. Investigators queried local authorities (*curacas*), as well as curers, 'witches', and other diviners and religious specialists concerning the persistence of the worship of ancestral mummies and sacred places in the landscape, such as mountains, caves, and springs. These documents are rich sources of information for contextualizing accounts of myths, as well as descriptions of similar beliefs and practices among the Incas, as recounted in earlier sources. In addition, the idolatrías provide testimony of the continuing religious persecution of native men and women in the Andean countryside during the colonial era.

Paqcha – painted wooden device used in performing divinations (Colonial Period).

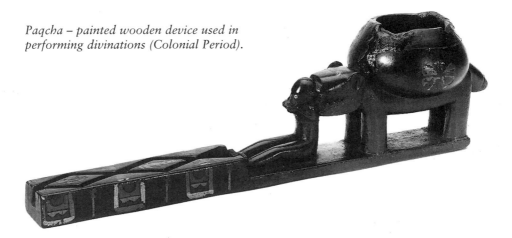

The local, state and cosmic themes uniting Inca myths

One of the most salient facts of life in the pre-Columbian Andes was the great ethnic diversity characterizing the subjects of the Incas. Such diversity seems to have had at least two important consequences for the shape and substance of myths in the empire. One was that this diversity itself needed an explanation. Why were people so different in terms of their language, dress and other customs and habits? Did near, or even distant, neighbours who seemed so fundamentally different from one another have different origins? Or did all people in the empire have a single origin?

Answers to questions such as these, which are represented in the contents of the myths themselves, lead us to distinguish two quite distinct bodies of origin myths. On one level, peoples in different parts of the empire appear to have insisted on the distinctiveness of their individual origins, and the myths resulting from these locally based myths and ideologies of origin display a multiplicity of creator deities and places and times of origin. We have a few dozen such origin myths from various parts of the empire, including the Lake Titicaca region, the north coast of Peru, and the central and northern highlands of Peru. What is important to recognize is that such myths exist in sufficient numbers to assure us that peoples in different parts of the empire promoted their individual origin myth, and their unique place of origin in the landscape, as components of ayllu or ethnic group identity and unity.

The Spanish priests and chroniclers had little patience with this notion of multiple places of origin. For instance, Bernabé Cobo was clearly frustrated by the different ideas about creator deities and the many versions of origin myths which he encountered in Peru. He concluded that the reason these 'blind people' accepted all these different ideas and beliefs was that they never knew about the one, true God. Furthermore, he continued, 'another contributing factor was their lack of any kind of writing. If they had had a system of writing, they might not have made such dim-witted errors.'

Juan de Betanzos, writing a century before Cobo, concluded that the 'confusion' was due to a more sinister cause, namely, the devil. As he put the matter, 'sometimes they [the Indians] hold the Sun up as the creator, and other times they say it is Viracocha. Generally, in all the land and in each of its provinces, the devil has them confused. Everywhere that the devil showed up, he told them a thousand lies and delusions. Thus he had them deceived and blind.'

On another level, the high degree of ethnic diversity that existed throughout the empire seems to have provided a powerful stimulus for the development of myths portraying the diverse ayllus and ethnic groups as descendants of a single event of origin in ancestral times. That is, in order for the diverse peoples within the empire to begin to think of themselves as citizens of a single society, it was essential that there be a powerful story and image linking them together, projecting their histories from a common past towards a united future. This latter tendency, which was motivated by the political interests of the Inca state bureaucracy in promoting unity throughout the empire, is reflected in myths depicting an intimate connection between the origins of the Inca kings and certain basic characteristics of the imperial organization, such as the hierarchical ranking of kin groups. To support their claims that imperial structures were foreordained and sanctioned by supernatural force(s), the Inca mythographers and story-tellers linked the origin of the Inca kings to two powerful deities – a creator deity (for instance, Viracocha or Pachacamac) and the sun – as well as to a place of origin located near to Cusco, called Pacaritambo.

Finally, at the most general, inclusive level, peoples throughout the Andes, including the Incas, commonly identified Lake Titicaca and the site of Tiahuanaco as the principal place where the cosmos, including the sun, moon, stars and the ancestors of humans, was first brought into being. We will see these various aspects of Inca origin myths – the local, the state, and the cosmic – in the myths that follow.

Cosmic origin myths

Cosmic origins

The story of the origin of the world that was apparently most commonly told by Inca informants, especially in Cusco, centred on Lake Titicaca. Most versions of this origin myth start by asserting that, in the beginning of time, all was in darkness, as the sun, moon and stars had not yet been created. Into this primeval darkness there emerged the creator Viracocha, whose name may be glossed as 'sea fat', or 'sea foam'. In various versions the creator is called Con Ticci Viracocha, Thunupa Viracocha, and Viracocha Pachayachachic. Later, in our discussion of myths from the Inca

Lake Titicaca.

provinces, we will also recount certain coastal myths that identify the creator as Pachacamac ('maker of earth/time').

In this time and space of darkness, Viracocha, who is described by Betanzos as a lord who emerged from Lake Titicaca, came forth and created the first race of humanity. These first beings, whom some chroniclers identify as a race of giants, lived in the darkness for a period of time but then, for some unspecified reason, they angered Viracocha. Because of his anger and his disappointment with them, the creator brought the first age to an end by a flood and transformed these beings into stone. Remnants of this first age were present for all to see in Inca times, and today, in the stone sculptures at the site of Tiahuanaco, near Lake Titicaca.

Viracocha next set about creating another race of humanity. He began this second act of creation by first calling the sun, the moon and the stars to come forth from an island in Lake Titicaca. The Incas maintained an important shrine, the focus of an annual pilgrimage, on an island in Lake Titicaca that they recognized as the Island of the Sun. After creating the celestial luminaries and setting them in motion, Viracocha fashioned the second race of humanity. In one telling of this creation story (Betanzos), Viracocha began by moulding individuals out of the stone along the shores of the lake, which was still malleable

Stone statue at Tiahuanaco.

Inca society before the time of the Spanish conquest, we may never be able to resolve this question with any degree of certainty.

Works of the creator in and around Cusco

In the versions of this origin myth recorded in the 1550s by Cieza de León and Juan de Betanzos, there is considerably more attention given to events that transpired in the central highlands as Con Ticci Viracocha travelled north-westward from Lake Titicaca. For instance, Cieza says that the creator, who had the appearance of a tall white man, travelled along the highland route healing the sick and restoring sight to the blind by his words alone. However, when Viracocha approached a village called Cacha, in the district of Canas (south-east of Cusco), the people came out of the town in a threatening manner, saying they were going to stone him. Betanzos says the people rushed at Viracocha with weapons.

Viracocha dropped to his knees and raised his hands toward the sky, as if seeking aid. The sky immediately filled with fire, and the terrified people of Cacha approached Viracocha, asking him to forgive and save them. The fire was then extinguished (Betanzos says that the creator gave the fire three strokes with his staff), but not before it had burned the rocks around there so that large blocks were consumed and became as light as cork. Betanzos says that he himself travelled to Cacha to investigate this mythic incident and clearly saw the scorched earth resulting from this cataclysmic event.

Betanzos elaborates on the repercussions of the creator's acts in and around this town, noting that the people of Cacha began to recognize the place where this event occurred as a *huaca*, or sacred place. They built a large stone sculpture in the shape of a man at the site where Viracocha appeared, and offered gold and silver to the huaca and statue. Betanzos is quite detailed and specific in describing the physical appearance of the creator, as this topic was apparently of considerable interest to him. That is, he not only tells us that he actually saw the statue of Viracocha himself, but also that he talked to people thereabouts, asking them what Viracocha looked like. Betanzos was told that 'he [Viracocha] was a tall man dressed in a white garment that reached to his ankles and was belted at the waist. His hair was short and he had a tonsure like a priest. He went bareheaded and carried in his hands something that seemed to them to resemble the breviaries that priests of today carry.' Betanzos says that the people around Cacha told him that the creator's name was Contiti Viracocha Pachayachachic, which he translates as 'God, maker of the world'.

Continuing his description of the events that transpired during Viracocha's travels north-westward, in the direction of Cusco from Lake Titicaca, Betanzos says that the creator next went to the site of Urcos, located six leagues (*c.* 33 km) from Cusco. Arriving there, Viracocha climbed to the top of a high mountain, sat down on the summit, and called the ancestors of the peoples who were native to that region in Betanzos' time to come out of the mountain-top. In homage to the time when the creator sat atop this mountain, the people of Urcos built a bench of gold there and placed a statue of Viracocha upon it. Molina tells us that the image of Viracocha at Urcos was called *Atun-Viracocha* ('great creator') and that the statue was in the form of a man with a white robe hanging down to his feet.

From Urcos, Viracocha passed on to Cusco. Here, in the place that would become the Inca capital, he created, or called up out of the earth, a great lord, whom he named Alcavicça. This name will reappear later as the name of the indigenous nation of people who were living in the valley of Cusco when the Incas first arrived there. In fact, Viracocha's last act upon leaving the valley of Cusco was to order that the so-called *orejones* – meaning 'big ears', the name given to the Inca nobility from their practice of piercing their earlobes and inserting golden spools in the holes – should emerge from the earth after he left. This final act in Cusco provides the link (in Betanzos' account) between the origin myth beginning at Lake Titicaca and the origin myth of the Inca kings.

The origin myth centring on Lake Titicaca contains several features which suggest strongly that its point of orientation was Cusco and its focus of validation was the hierarchical structures underlying the Inca state. For instance, the space traversed by characters in the myth begins at the lake and proceeds north-westward to the coast of Ecuador. The more detailed narration of encounters between the creator and people – those occurring in Cacha and Urcos – centre on the Vilcanota, or Urubamba river valley, which courses north-westward near Cusco and within the Cusco valley itself. Thus the myths of the origins of the world told by informants in the Inca capital project a vital connection between Lake Titicaca, the site of one of the principal highland civilizations of pre-Inca times (Tiahuanaco), and Cusco, the successor capital.

The origin myths we have discussed thus far pay curiously little attention to what would become the major geographic, demographic and political division defining the Inca world, that of *Tahuantinsuyu*, 'the four united quarters'. An especially puzzling omission in the origin myths concerns the quadrant of Collasuyu. This quarter of the empire, which included the territory south-east of Cusco, extended not only from the capital to Lake Titicaca but also much farther to the south-east, into central and southern Bolivia and on into north-west Argentina. Now, if the work of creation proceeded from Lake Titicaca to the *north-west*, what were the origins of the peoples of Collasuyu, to the south-east of Lake Titicaca? Were the powerful nations and confederations of nations of Bolivia (the QaraQara and Charka, for example) not created at the same time and in the same manner as those of the other three quarters of Tahuantinsuyu? There is no body of myths that would settle our unease about the Inca disregard of this portion of the empire. One possibility suggested is that the Incas may have taken over and remoulded – that is, retold from the point of view of Cusco – the myths of Collasuyu itself, hoping thereby to incorporate into their own origins the power and legitimacy associated even in those times with the mighty kingdoms and confederations of what is today Bolivia.

One myth that does account for the division of the Inca world into four quarters at the beginning of time is provided by Garcilaso de la Vega in his work, *Commentarios Reales de los Incas*. Garcilaso says that after the waters of the deluge receded, a man (unnamed in this myth) appeared at Tiahuanaco. This man was so powerful that he divided the land into four parts, giving each quarter to one of four kings. Manco Capac received the northern quarter, Colla the southern, Tocay the eastern, and Pinahua the western. This 'creator' of Tiahuanaco commanded each king to enter the quarter assigned to him and to conquer and govern the people who lived there.

We would be well served at this point by summarizing some of the key elements that have appeared in the myths discussed so far. These represent what could be characterized as core, or paradigmatic, ideas, events and relationships that will reappear with striking regularity as we turn to the myths of other places in the empire, especially along the spine of the Andes from Bolivia northward to Ecuador. Because of their widespread distribution in both time and space, they could well represent indigenous – that is, pre-conquest – concepts and thematic principles informing, and giving shape and unity to, mythological traditions throughout the empire.

The first paradigmatic element is the notion that all humanity (within the empire, at least) originated at Lake Titicaca, urged into being there by a supreme creator most commonly identified as Viracocha. Second, one consistently finds that the particular group of people – a 'nation', ayllu or family – occupying a given region will recognize a particular place in the local landscape, such as a spring or cave, as its unique place of origin. Offerings will be made to the place, which will be regarded as a huaca ('sacred place'), for the well-being of the group as a whole. In addition, the mummified ancestors of the group may be stored and worshipped there. The third element is a complementary relationship, which may be either co-operative or more commonly conflictual in nature, between this local autochthonous group of people and a group of outsiders who are believed to have arrived on the scene in the past as conquering invaders. The resulting relationship between locals and foreigners is the defining one for political life within the territory occupied by the two groups. The final paradigmatic element is a principle of ranking, or hierarchy, that suffuses all relationships among peoples, places and histories across the landscape. As we continue, we will see these paradigmatic elements reappear in myths from throughout the empire with notable regularity. For the moment, it is important to examine another theme that underlies the cosmic views of colonial commentators on the Incas.

Pachacuti: cycles of creation and destruction in myths of the ages of the world

A central concept in Inca and later colonial Quechua and Aymara cosmogonic thinking was the notion of regular episodes of the cataclysmic destruction and recreation of the world. This notion is evident in the myths in a general theme of cyclicity that characterizes the succession of events in mythic times.

The cyclical concept is evoked in the Quechua term *pachacuti*, which refers to a 'revolution, or turning over/around' (*cuti*) of 'time and space' (*pacha*). Pachacuti is the term that is often used in chroniclers' accounts of the numerous mythic episodes of the destruction of the inhabitants of the world and their replacement by a new race, as we have seen in some of the origin myths from Lake Titicaca. This theme is well-represented in the corpus of Inca myths collected during the colonial period, one of the best examples being that given by Guaman Poma de Ayala in his *Nueva Corónica y Buen Gobierno*.

Guaman Poma's mid-seventeenth century version of the world depicts a succession of five ages. From comparison with other versions, it appears that the general scheme in the Inca/Andean cosmic vision was of five ages, each referred to as a 'sun' and with each sun/age enduring for a thousand years.

In Guaman Poma's version, the first age began during a time of primordial darkness with a race of humanity called *Wari Wiracocharuna*. The term *wari* refers to a hybrid camellid, a cross-breeding between a llama and an alpaca; *runa* is the Quechua term for 'people'. Guaman Poma glosses this name as the people from the time of Noah's ark who were descended from Spaniards (in addition to its designation of the creator deity, 'Viracocha' was used by Andean natives to refer to the invading Europeans). The people of the first age lived with only rudimentary technology and wore clothing of leaves and other unprocessed vegetal materials. Guaman Poma says that the Wari Wiracocharuna first worshipped God, but they then lost faith and began worshipping Andean creator deities, including two forms of Viracocha – Ticci Viracocha and Caylla Viracocha – and Pachacamac. The first age came to an end in some unspecified manner.

The second race of humanity, called *Wari Runa*, was more advanced than the previous race. The Wari Runa had clothing of animal skins; they practised rudimentary agriculture and lived simply and peacefully, without warfare. They recognized Viracocha as their creator. The second age ended in a deluge.

The third age was that of the *Purun Runa* ('wild men'). Civilization was becoming increasingly complex, as witnessed by the fact that the people of this age made clothing of spun and dyed wool; they practised agriculture, mining and the making of jewellery. The population grew beyond previous levels, with people migrating into the previously uninhabited lowlands. There was a marked increase in conflicts and warfare. Each town had its own king, and the people as a whole worshipped the creator Pachacamac.

The fourth age was that of the 'warlike people', the *Auca Runa*. In certain passages, Guaman Poma suggests that the early part of the Inca empire fell within this age, but elsewhere the Incas are considered to have lived during the fifth age. During the age of the Auca Runa, the world was divided into four parts. Warfare increased, and people lived on mountaintops in stone houses and fortifications, called *pucaras*. Ayllus became common in this age, and decimal administration was instituted. In general, the technological and material conditions of life became far more advanced

The first four ages of the world, according to Guaman Poma de Ayala.

TER3ERAEDADDEIÑS
PVRVNRVNA

ELQVARTOEDADDEIÑS
AVCARVNA

and complex than in the previous age. Guaman Poma does not specify how this age ended.

The fifth age, or 'sun', was that of the Incas. In his chronicle, Guaman Poma gives a description of the major institutions of the empire, including the institution of the kingship, the decimal bureaucracy, the age-grades of the population and the religious organization of the empire. With respect to the latter, the Incas began the worship of what Guaman Poma refers to as the *guaca bilcas*, the supernaturals who were, as he says, 'the demons of Cusco'. The fifth age was brought to an end, of course, by the Spanish conquest.

This brief overview of Guaman Poma's construction of the five ages or 'suns' omits many of the details of what is, in fact, a complex and rather confusing account. Guaman Poma mixes many Christian symbols and sentiments with what appear to be indigenous elements. The latter include references to the creator deities Viracocha and Pachacamac, whom we have encountered before; institutions that are long-attested in the Andes, such as ayllus and decimal organization and an overall structure built around the notion of a succession of pachacutis – creations and destructions of the world. As we will see later, this concept persists in contemporary Andean myths, especially in those concerning the end of the present world and the anticipated reinstatement of the Incas as the rightful rulers of the land.

These comments and the earlier description of the place of the Incas in the five ages of the world prompt us to ask: Who were the Incas? Where did they come from? Answers to these questions were of vital interest not only to the Incas, but also to the Spanish chroniclers, who struggled to make sense of what they perceived to be the bewildering set of events that occurred at the beginning of time as recounted in Andean cosmic origin myths.

Origin myths of the Inca state

arly in his account of the origin of the Incas, the Jesuit priest Bernabé Cobo alerts us to the fact that, unlike other lineages or ethnic groups in the Andes, the Incas – perhaps because they recognized the political danger involved – were not content with the situation in which every local group had its own place of origin, each one as important as the next. For them, their place of origin was special, and all-inclusive. As Cobo noted, 'The reason why these nations of Peru came to believe so much nonsense about their origin was caused by the ambition of the Incas. They were the first one to worship the cave of Pacaritampu as the beginning of their lineage. They claimed that all people came from there, and that for this reason all people were their vassals and obliged to serve them.' Clearly, the Inca had other ambitions in mind in recounting their myth of origin from the cave of Pacaritambo.

In outline form, the origin myth of the Incas focusing on Pacaritambo is as follows: At a place to the south of Cusco called Pacaritambo, there was a mountain called Tambo T'oco ('window house'), in which there were three windows, or caves. The ancestors of the Incas, who were related as a group of four brothers and four sisters, came out of the central window. The principal figure was Manco Capac, who was destined to become the founder-king of the empire. The Incas set off with people who lived around Tambo T'oco in search of fertile land on which to build their capital. Following a long period of wandering, they finally arrived at a hill overlooking the valley of Cusco. Recognizing by miraculous signs that this was the home they had long sought, the Incas descended from the mountain and took possession of the valley from the local inhabitants.

The principal account that I shall use in elaborating the Inca origin myth is the version given in Sarmiento de Gamboa's *Historia de los Incas*, which was written in 1572. Sarmiento's account is one of the earliest and most detailed versions that we have. As the official historian to Francisco de Toledo, the fourth Viceroy of Peru (1569-81), Sarmiento was charged with compiling a true history of the Inca empire. In undertaking this enterprise, Sarmiento had access to an unusually large number of informants. He tells us, for instance, that he interviewed more than a hundred quipucamayoqs on historical matters, and he provides us with the names of forty-two of these informants. Furthermore, Sarmiento says that upon completing his account, he had his chronicle read in full, in the Quechua language, to these forty-two descendants of the Inca nobility. All of the men, says Sarmiento, agreed that 'the said history was good and true and conformed to what they knew and to what they had heard their parents and ancestors say, which they themselves had heard their own [parents and ancestors] say.' As we will see, much of the 'true history' recorded by Sarmiento falls decidedly under the heading of what we generally classify as mythology.

According to Sarmiento, the origin of the Incas was at a place called Pacaritambo ('the inn, or house, of dawn'; or 'place of origin'), which is located six leagues (c. 33 km) south of Cusco. In primordial times, there was a mountain at Pacaritambo called Tambo Toco ('the house of openings/windows') in which there were three windows, or caves. The central window was called Capac Toco ('rich window'), and the two lateral windows were called Maras Toco and Sutic Toco. Two different nations of Indians who allied themselves with the Incas originated from these side windows. A nation called the Maras emerged from the window of Maras Toco, while the Tambos Indians (whose head lineage seems to have borne the surname Sutic) came out of the window of Sutic Toco. The ancestors of the Incas emerged from the central window, Capac Toco. Sarmiento says that these three groups of people were born from the caves, or windows, of Tambo Toco at the urging of Ticci Viracocha.

From the central window at Tambo Toco there emerged four men and four women who were, according to Sarmiento, brothers and sisters. Betanzos says that the ancestors were paired as spouses. The names of the eight ancestral siblings as given by Sarmiento in the order of their age-grading (with the oldest pair, Ayar Manco and Mama Ocllo, listed first) were:

The Inca king and queen worshipping the cave of Tambo Toco at Pacaritambo.

Brothers/Husbands	Sisters/Wives
Ayar Manco (Capac)	Mama Ocllo
Ayar Auca	Mama Huaco
Ayar Cachi	Mama Ipacura/Cura
Ayar Uchu	Mama Raua

'Ayar' comes from the Quechua word *aya*, 'corpse', thereby establishing a link between the ancestors as mythological characters and the mummified remains of the Inca kings, which were kept and worshipped in a special room in the Temple of the Sun in Cusco. In addition, this same word *ayar* was the name of a wild strain of the *quinua* plant, a high-altitude grain crop of the Andes.

We should note that while all accounts of the Ayars say that the ancestors came from Tambo Toco at Pacaritambo, in the chronicles of Martín de Murúa and Guaman Poma de Ayala we read that the ancestors originally passed underground from Lake Titicaca to the cave of Pacaritambo. In addition, Garcilaso de la Vega included in his chronicle the Inca origin myth that links Manco Capac and Mama Ocllo to the Island of the Sun, in Lake Titicaca.

After the ancestors emerged from Tambo Toco, they allied themselves with the Tambos Indians and prepared to go with them in search of fertile land; upon finding good land, they vowed to conquer the people who lived there. Sarmiento describes this turn of events as follows:

'And agreeing among themselves on this [plan for conquest], the eight [ancestors] began to stir up the people who lived in that part of the mountain, setting as the prize that they [the Inca ancestors] would make the people rich and that they would give them the lands and estates which they conquered and subjugated. From an interest in this [proposition], there were formed ten groups or ayllus, which means, among these barbarians, a lineage or faction.'

The first Inca king, Manco Capac.

The ten ayllus of Tambos Indians founded at Tambo Toco were destined to become the principal groupings of commoners in Inca Cusco. They were complemented in the social organization of the capital by the ten royal ayllus, called *panacas*, which were composed of the descendants of the first ten kings. Shortly after their creation and emergence from Tambo Toco, the eight ancestors set off with their entourage – the ten ayllus of Tambos Indians – walking northward in the direction of the Cusco valley. Along the way, the ancestors tested the earth by plunging a golden bar, which they had brought with them from Tambo Toco, into the soil. They were searching for fertile land that would be suitable to call home.

The ancestors made several stops along their journey to Cusco. During the first of these stops the oldest brother, Ayar Manco (who will later be called Manco Capac), and his sister/wife, Mama Ocllo, conceived a child. At the second stop, Mama Ocllo gave birth to a boy, whom they named Sinchi Roca. This child was destined to succeed his father (Ayar Manco) as second king of Cusco. In Betanzos' version of the Inca origin myth, he says that Sinchi Roca was born in Cusco, after the ancestors had reached and taken possession of the city. From the second stop, in Sarmiento's version, the group then moved on to a place called Palluta, where they remained for a few years. However, becoming dissatisfied with the land there, they decided to move on. The ancestors and their entourage then came to a place called Haysquisrro. It was here that a momentous event occurred that resulted in the separation of one of the ancestors from the group.

According to various versions of the Inca origin myth, Ayar Cachi was known universally as a boisterous, rowdy and cruel character; he was also very handy with a sling. Cieza tells us that Ayar Cachi could launch stones from his sling with such force that he could split hills, the rocks and dust flying up to the clouds. In addition, Ayar Cachi stirred up trouble in all the towns the ancestors passed through, and he disturbed the peace and harmony among the ancestors and their allies. According to Sarmiento, 'the other siblings feared that because of his bad behavior and tricks, Ayar Cachi would disturb and alienate the people who were travelling with them, and that they [the ancestors] would be left alone.'

These concerns led the ancestors, under the direction of Ayar Manco, to concoct a ruse to rid themselves of this troublesome character. Manco told Ayar Cachi that they had left several items in the cave of origin, Tambo Toco. These included a golden cup (*topacusi*), some seeds, as well as an object called a *napa*. The latter had the form of a miniature decorative llama, which, in Sarmiento's words, was an 'insignia of nobility'. (Molina gives numerous examples of ceremonies in Cusco during which the Incas brought out, and worshipped, small images of llamas made of gold and silver.) At first, Ayar Cachi refused to return to the cave. However, Mama Huaco, the most forceful and bellicose of the sisters (and according to Betanzos the wife of Ayar Cachi), jumped to her feet and began berating Ayar Cachi, calling him a lazy coward. Shamed into action by Mama Huaco's words, Ayar Cachi agreed to return to the cave.

On his trip back to Tambo Toco, Ayar Cachi took with him a man from

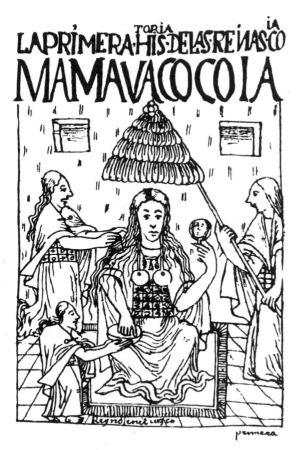

LAPRIMERA·HISTORIA·DELAS·RE·YNA·CO
MAMAVACOCOIA

Mama Huaco.

among the Tambos Indians, named Tambochacay ('Tambo entrance-barrer'). Unbeknownst to Ayar Cachi, the other ancestors had persuaded Tambochacay to dispose of the troublesome Ayar Cachi when they reached the cave. Arriving at Tambo Toco, Ayar Cachi went inside to retrieve the articles. Tambochacay immediately closed off the entrance to the cave with a huge boulder, trapping Ayar Cachi inside for all time.

Having rid themselves of Ayar Cachi, the ancestors moved on and arrived next in the immediate environs of the valley of Cusco at a place called Quirirmanta, which is at the foot of a mountain called Huanacauri. Ascending Huanacauri, the ancestors viewed for the first time the valley of Cusco. Heaving the bar of gold with which they had been testing the soil into the valley, they saw the entire shaft sink into the earth. From this indication, as well as by the sign of a rainbow that stretched over the valley, the ancestors recognized that this was their long sought-after home and they prepared to descend.

At this point, the youngest of the ancestor-brothers, Ayar Uchu, was transformed into stone on the mountain Huanacauri. In Betanzos' version of this myth, he tells us that before his transformation into stone, Ayar Uchu stood up on the mountain, spread out a pair of large wings, and flew from the top of the mountain into the heavens. On his return, he said that he had

The view from atop Huanacauri, looking into the Cusco valley.

talked to the sun who told him that Ayar Manco should from that moment on be called Manco Capac ('supreme rich [one]') and that the entourage should proceed to Cusco. There, said Ayar Uchu, the Incas would find good company in the place where Alcavicça had his settlement. After saying these things, Ayar Uchu was transformed into stone. The Incas later worshipped this stone as one of their principal sacred sites (huacas).

The remaining six ancestors went from Huanacauri to a place called Matao, where Sarmiento says they remained for two years. Betanzos recounts an event that occurred at about this same point in the ancestral journey but at an unnamed place (perhaps Matao?) near Cusco, which was famous for coca and *aji* (chili peppers). Here Mama Huaco, who was herself quite skilful with a sling, struck a man of the town with a stone flung from her sling and killed him. She then split open his chest, took out his lungs and heart, blew into the lungs, making them swell up, and displayed them to the inhabitants of the town. The people fled, and the ancestors proceeded on to Cusco.

Arriving there, they went up to Alcavicça and told him they had been sent there by their father, the sun, to take possession of the town. Alcavicça and his followers acceded to this request and made room for the six ancestors. Then Manco Capac took some maize (corn) seeds that he had brought with him from the cave of Tambo Toco, and with the help of Alcavicça and the other ancestors he planted the first corn field in the valley. Molina gives an interesting account of this final act whereby

Inca vessel composed of replicas of aryballos, ear of corn and digging stick.

the Incas 'domesticated' the valley of Cusco by planting their fields there. He says this field was first planted not by Manco Capac but by Mama Huaco, one of the ancestral sisters. After Mama Huaco died, her body was embalmed and mummified, and the people who were responsible for caring for her mummy made *chicha* (fermented corn beer) from the corn grown every year in this same field; the chicha was given to those who maintained the cult of the mummy of Mama Huaco.

When Manco Capac and his companions finally reached the place that would become the centre of the city of Cusco, the plaza of Huanaypata, Ayar Auca – the only remaining ancestor brother besides Manco Capac – was transformed into a stone pillar. This pillar was worshipped from that time on as a huaca. This left Manco Capac, his four sisters and the boy Sinchi Roca to found and build the city of Cusco.

To recapitulate, in the versions of the Inca origin myth recounted by Sarmiento, Betanzos and other chroniclers, we encounter the various motifs characterized earlier as 'paradigmatic elements' of origin myths in the empire. That is, the ancestors, who initially came underground from Lake Titicaca, had their unique place of origin in the cave of Tambo Toco, in Pacaritambo. This cave, where one of the ancestors, Ayar Cachi, remained entombed, was recognized as an important huaca and pilgrimage site in Inca times. (The ruins of the site are known today as Mauqallaqta, 'ancient town'.) The ancestors went from the cave of origin to the valley of Cusco where, in conquering the local, autochthonous people under the command of Alcavicça, they established the core, hier-archical, political relationship between foreign invaders and local subordinates that came to characterize relations between the Incas in the capital and local peoples throughout the empire from this time forward.

Was the Inca state founded on a ruse?

Before we move on to examine other mythic events that supposedly transpired in Cusco after the conquest of the valley by Manco Capac, we should first examine another tradition of Inca origins from Pacaritambo that projects Inca motives as decidedly more sinister and duplicitous. The basic story-line of this version is that the Ayar siblings decided among themselves

The site of Mauqallaqta, Inca Pacaritambo (left).

to trick the local people of the valley of Cusco into believing that they (the Inca ancestors) were descended from the sun. Manco Capac then fashioned, or had fashioned for him, two plates of gold, one of which he wore on the front of his body, the other on his back. Manco then positioned himself on the hill of Huanacauri overlooking Cusco where, at the moment of sunrise, he appeared as a resplendent, god-like figure. The locals were awed by his appearance, whereupon Manco descended from Huanacauri to Cusco and took command of the valley.

Different versions of this story derive from various sources. Depending on the source, the 'trick' which the ancestors played on the locals can sound exceedingly clever (as it does, for instance, in the version by Martín de Murúa); at its worst, however, the ruse has a sinister undertone, one which implies that the whole rule of the Incas was illegitimate by virtue of this act of trickery played on the people. In this regard, we should specifically note an account of the origin of the Incas contained in testimony given before Vaca de Castro in Cusco, in about 1542, only ten years after the Spanish conquest. This appears in the document called the *Relación de los Quipucamayoqs*, which was drawn up from the testimony provided by four elderly quipucamayoqs, two of whom are said to have been natives of the town of Pacaritambo. The particular version of the origin myth that was apparently told by the two quipucamayoqs from Pacaritambo goes as follows.

Manco Capac was the son of a *curaca* (a local official and head of a high-ranking lineage) of Pacaritambo. Manco's mother had died at the time of his birth, and the boy grew up with his father. When Manco was a boy, his father called him by the nickname 'Son of the Sun'. When Manco reached the age of ten or twelve, his father died. However, since his father had not explained to Manco Capac that the name 'Son of the Sun' was only an innocent nickname, Manco and the 'stupid people' (*gente bruta*) of the town were left with the idea that he was actually the son of the sun. Now, in Manco's household there were two old men, who were the priests of the idols of Manco Capac's father. These men continued to promote the 'hoax' (*patraña*) that Manco was a divine being. Manco Capac came to accept these pretensions, and when he reached the age of eighteen or twenty, he became further convinced by the two priests that he and his descendants were the

Manco Capac standing atop Huanacauri.

natural lords of the earth. Animated by these pretensions, Manco Capac made ready to set off for Cusco, taking with him the other members of his family, the two old priests, as well as his father's principal idol, which was called Huanacauri. This version of the deceitful co-optation of power by the Incas ends like the other version discussed above, with Manco Capac standing on the mountain of Huanacauri dressed in splendid fashion, bedecked with gold, and dazzling the people into accepting him and his family as their rulers.

The chronicler Garcilaso de la Vega added a further twist to the origin myth of the Incas by linking Manco Capac both to Lake Titicaca and to the theme of the first Inca's deceptive identification of himself as child of the sun. Garcilaso says that Manco Capac was aware that the people at Lake Titicaca believed that, following the great deluge, the sun had first shone its light on the Island of the Sun. Knowing this, he made up a fable to the effect that the sun placed his two children, one male and one female, there to teach the 'barbarous' Indians thereabouts how to live in a civilized manner. 'With these and other inventions made for their benefit, the Incas induced the remaining Indians to believe they were the children of the sun and confirmed it by the good they did.'

Stories such as these present the modern reader with the greatest challenges in separating what may have been Inca beliefs and what may have represented events or sentiments imputed to the Incas by their European, and/or Christian commentators. For example, the notion that the fame, prestige and power of Manco Capac, and by extension that of his regal descendants, rested on a ruse, hoax or a trick played on the people looks, on one level, like a politically interested manipulation of the origin myth by those who wanted to call into question the legitimacy of Inca rule. On another level, which may have had some force in the case of Garcilaso de la Vega, those who professed Christianity would have been inclined to see the workings of the devil in native worship of the sun. Thus there would have been in this latter case a profound suspicion of the devil's work in the events that led to the ascendence of the Incas, as 'children of the sun'. Whatever the specific motives and interests of the various chroniclers who recount these myths, there is a sufficient and varied number of sources pointing to solar worship in the Inca empire that we cannot doubt the antiquity and pervasiveness of such beliefs.

A more troublesome and difficult issue concerns the chronological relationship between the worship of Viracocha and the worship of the sun. Some chroniclers suggest that the Inca worship of the sun was a late development, coming only after the expansion of the empire beyond the boundaries of the valley of Cusco and with the maturity of the imperial bureaucratic organization. Others argue that the worship of Viracocha superseded the worship of the sun. Again, the lack of good chronological controls on Inca event chronologies as a whole renders answers to such questions highly speculative.

Myths of Inca state consolidation and expansion

In the mythic history of the Incas outlined thus far, we have followed those accounts that chronicle the events and processes whereby the first Inca, Manco Capac, and his brothers and sisters came to dominate affairs in the valley of Cusco. All subsequent kings of the empire, whether succeeding each other in a single line of succession, as some students of Inca history believe, or whether succession was in dual, co-regal lines, as other students hold, were ultimately descendants of the first king, Manco Capac, and his sister-wife, Mama Ocllo.

We are confronted by a complex set of questions in regard to the succession of the Inca kings following Manco Capac. This includes such issues as, first, the total number of kings that ruled from the accession of Manco Capac until the arrival of the Spaniards in 1532; second, the dates of the reigns of the various kings; and third, whether or not the kings were actual historical persons, or if some (or all?) of them should be relegated to the realm of mythology. We cannot, nor do we need to, enter into all the subtleties and nuances of the various opinions held by scholars on these questions. Rather, as a basis for our discussion of selected mythical events recounted in various of the sources concerning the consolidation of power by the Incas within the valley of Cusco, we can refer to the following list of generally well-attested kings of the empire. Most accounts aver that the last, undisputed Inca to rule before the Spanish conquest was Guayna Capac. At the time of the entry of the Spanish into Peru, succession to the throne was being disputed between two of Guayna Capac's sons (by different women), Huascar and Atahualpa.

The kings of the Inca empire

Manco Capac

Sinchi Roca

Lloque Yupanqui

Mayta Capac

Capac Yupanqui

Inca Roca

Yahuar Huacac

Viracocha Inca

Pachacuti Inca Yupanqui

Tupac Inca Yupanqui

Guayna Capac

Huascar and Atahualpa

The chroniclers give varying amounts and types of information about the different kings and queens of the empire. Some of this information is highly plausible, and the events referred to must have occurred at some time, under one king or another, in the late pre-conquest period. For instance, Manco Capac was said to have divided the population of Cusco into two parts that came to be referred to as 'upper Cusco' (*Hanan Cusco*) and 'lower Cusco' (*Hurin Cusco*), and the populace of the city was indeed divided in this manner at the time of the arrival of the Spanish. Sinchi Roca was said to have commanded people in the valley to cultivate the land for producing potatoes, and the valley has been so cultivated from at least Inca times until the present day. Finally, Mayta Capac was said to have quelled a rebellion by the Alcaviçças, who had become restless by the time of his reign. All of these events or actions are plausible historical occurrences, although we cannot say precisely when any one of them may actually have occurred.

On the other hand, such events as those outlined above are jumbled together in the various sources with events that are decidedly more mythical in nature. Here, we should remark in particular two events that I will call 'mythic-historical' (as we cannot be certain of their historical status), for they appear to have been of great importance in Inca informants' accounts of the emergence of the Incas and the consolidation of the empire. The first concerns the war against the Chancas, a powerful nation to the west of Cusco; the second concerns an encounter between a young Inca prince and the creator god, Viracocha.

The attack on Cusco by the Chanca armies and the defence of the city by a young prince was of profound significance in Inca mythic history, for it is said that it was only after this event that the Incas set themselves on the road to building an empire. Some sources say the hero-prince of this myth was Viracocha Inca, the son of Yahuar Huacac, while others credit the event to Viracocha Inca's son, Pachacuti Inca Yupanqui. As the Chanca troops began advancing on the city, most of the residents, including the king, fled. Only the young prince and a few companions remained to defend Cusco. The few defenders were almost defeated in the first two attacks launched by the Chancas; however, in the final attack, with the fate of the Incas in the balance, the young prince received the aid of the rocks and stones in the valley, which were transformed into warriors. The rocks, called *pururaucas*, were worshipped as huacas from that time onward.

The tone and substance of the different versions of this myth in the various chronicles give the modern reader – as they must have given the Inca listener – the sense that the achievement of Inca sovereignty in the valley, a process which set them on the trajectory of empire, received divine sanction when the very stones of the valley rose up to protect the Incas and defend the city. In addition, it is at this point in the mythic-history of Cusco, and particularly in the recounting of the deeds of the various kings, that some scholars argue that our information in the colonial documents makes the transition from primarily mythical to historical. This view credits Pachacuti Inca with the defeat of the Chancas, and it is thought that this event was followed by a significant consolidation and expansion of the city of Cusco and the empire. According to this view, the dates of Pachacuti's reign are given as AD 1438–71. So far, this historicized interpretation of Inca dynastic mythic-histories has not been confirmed by any supporting archaeological data.

Another view of these events, which also regards at least certain elements of the Chanca war as 'real' history, although it does not attempt to attach absolute dates to these elements, suggests that this conflict may actually represent a deep, essentially historical, memory of the Inca rise to power in the Cusco valley. The principal, defining event of this process would have been the Inca defeat of the remnants of Huari control in the Cusco valley. The homeland of the Huari peoples, who were the central Peruvian contemporaries in Middle Horizon times of the Tiahuanaco peoples of Lake Titicaca, was located in the general area where the Chanca peoples were said to have had their seat of power.

To return to the myths of Inca state formation, another signal, mythic event recounted in the chronicles during the same (relative) time period as that subsumed by the Chanca war involved the encounter between the young prince Pachacuti Inca Yupanqui and the creator Viracocha Pachayachachi. This occurred at a spring outside Cusco, called Susurpuquio. As Pachacuti approached the spring on a journey to visit his father, Viracocha Inca, he saw a crystal tablet fall into it. The prince looked into the spring, and he saw on the tablet the image of an Indian wearing a *llauto* (a headdress), earspools and clothing like those worn by the Incas. It had three rays, like those of the sun, emerging from its head and snakes coiled around its shoulders. The figure had the head of a 'lion' (puma) jutting forward between its legs, another lion on its back with its paws around its shoulders and a serpent-like creature that stretched from the top to the bottom of its back.

Pachacuti took the crystal with him when he left the spring, and he used it from that time onward to see into the future. Pachacuti was said later to have come to identify the image on the crystal tablet with the creator, Viracocha Pachayachachi. The prince was so impressed by this vision that he was said to have instituted a religious reform during the time of his reign. In this particular accounting of the hierarchy of deities in the empire (there were other, competing versions), it is said that from the time of the Inca Pachacuti Yupanqui onward, the main temple of ritual and worship in the city of Cusco, the Coricancha, was reorganized to accommodate and display the following hierarchy of gods: Viracocha, the Sun, Moon, Venus, Thunder and the Rainbow. This hierarchy resulted from the replacement of the Sun, which had previously been the supreme deity and image in Coricancha and in the Inca pantheon, by Viracocha, the patron deity of Pachacuti, the new king.

However, another version of the evolution of Inca religion in connection with Pachacuti Yupanqui asserts that this king was responsible for what has been termed the increasing 'solarization' of Inca religion in which the sun replaced Viracocha as the principal deity of the empire. According to this point of view, Pachacuti's rise to power, during which he replaced his father, who bore the name 'Viracocha', was symbolic of this fundamental shift away from the worship of Viracocha to that of the Sun. One topic that is centrally at issue in this controversy is the fact that one of the kings, Viracocha Inca, bore the same name, or title, as the creator. This is account-ed for, in Betanzos' chronicle, for instance, by the fact that Viracocha Inca claimed that the creator appeared before him one night when he, the king, was troubled. The creator calmed him and made him content. The next day, when the king reported this event to his subjects, they stood up and pro-claimed his name to be Viracocha Inca, 'which means king and god'.

Much ink has been spilled over the question of the relationship between Viracocha the creator and Viracocha the king. We cannot resolve the issue here, nor can we easily make the problem go away. This is one area where the mixing, or 'confusion', between myth and history is quite perplexing and, given the nature of our sources (with different chroniclers speaking to different informants at different times and receiving different accounts and explanations), one that may not be resolvable into an absolute separation of these two central characters in Inca mythology.

Questions such as these must have occupied the attention of successive generations of quipucamayoqs and poet-philosophers (the amautas) in Cusco as they recounted, and even on occasion reformulated, myths of the Inca past. What most interested the people outside Cusco, however, although they retained myths concerning some of these imperial preoccupations, were questions regarding their own past. Where did they come from? How were neighbouring groups of people related to each other? And how, and when, did they come to be under the control of the Incas? We turn in the next chapter to some of the few bodies of myths that have been preserved for our appreciation and which address these and other provincial concerns.

Coastal and provincial mythologies

The lords of the north coast and the Incas

The myths of the Ayars and the founding of Cusco and the Inca empire are the principal myths of state origins we have from the Andes, but they are not the only ones. When we turn our attention elsewhere in the empire, particularly to the north coast of Peru, we encounter there tantalizing remnants of state origin myths altogether as complex as those of the Cusco dynasty. Unfortunately, we have only the barest outlines of a few of these myths, including a couple from the Lambayeque valley and one pertaining to the lords of Chimor, in the Moche valley.

Concerning the myths centring on Lambayeque, Cabello Balboa tells us in his chronicle from 1586 of a tradition concerning an invasion of this valley in primordial times by peoples from the sea, to the south, who arrived in a fleet of balsas, or rafts. The leader of what Cabello Balboa calls this 'brave and noble company' of men was a man named Naymlap. Naymlap was accompanied by his wife, Ceterni, a harem, and some forty attendants. The retinue included a trumpeter, a guardian of the royal litter, a man who ground conch shells into powder for ritual purposes, a cook, and many more special functionaries. Naymlap also brought with him a green stone idol, which bore the name Yampallec, a name that is thought to be the origin of the name of the river valley where Naymlap settled, Lambayeque. Cabello Balboa tells us that the idol Yampallec had the figure and stature of Naymlap, thus being the king's double. Naymlap built a palace and a centre of devotion for the green stone idol at a place called Chot. This is almost certainly the site of Huaca Chotuna in the Lambayeque valley.

Naymlap lived a long and peaceful life. When he died, his body was buried in the palace of Chot. However, Naymlap had arranged

Chimu paddle.

Reconstruction of an interior courtyard, Huaca Chotuna, Lambyeque valley.

with his priests that when he died, they should tell his followers that upon his death he took wings and flew away. Naymlap was succeeded by his eldest son, Cium, who married a woman named Zolzoloñi, apparently a local woman (i.e., she is referred to in the document as a *moza*, a common designation in Spanish for a woman from outside a particular, named group – in this case, the group of invaders from the south). Cium and Zolzoloñi had twelve sons, each of whom married, had a large family, and went off on their own to found a different city.

Beginning with Naymlap, there were twelve kings in this dynasty, the last of whom was named Fempellec. Fempellec decided to move the green stone idol, Yampallec, from Chot to a new site, but before he could carry this out, the devil (says Cabello Balboa) appeared to him in the form of a beautiful woman, who seduced him. Following Fempellec's seduction by this sorceress, it began raining – in a part of Peru where it seldom rains – and continued raining for thirty days. After this, a year of drought and hunger set in. At the end of the year, the priests of the green stone idol had had enough. They seized Fempellec, bound him hand and foot and threw him into the ocean – thus ended the dynasty of Naymlap of Lambayeque.

Continuing his recounting of events in the Lambayeque valley, Cabello Balboa then says that 'many days' after the death of Fempellec, Lambayeque was once again invaded by a powerful army from the sea. The leader of this army was a man named Chimo Capac ('lord Chimu'), a name or title which indicates his probable origins in the Moche valley, centre of the kingdom of Chimor. Chimo Capac took control of Lambayeque and installed his curaca (local lord), Pongmassa, in the valley. This man was succeeded by his son, and then by Pongmassa's grandson, during whose period of rule the Incas conquered the area. The valley then continued under Inca control through some five other curacas, who administered the valley on behalf of the Incas. The Inca-Chimu alliance came to an end with the arrival of the Spanish.

We learn elsewhere of another north coastal dynasty, that of Taycanamu, whose home was the Moche valley. Like Naymlap and Chimo Capac, Taycanamu arrived at Moche from the south, on a balsa raft. Several descendants of Taycanamu ruled in succession, each expanding the territory under his control until the sixth or seventh ruler, a man named Minchançaman, was conquered by an Inca lord, Topa Yupanqui. Minchançaman was taken to Cusco, and the Moche valley was effectively brought under Inca control and remained so until the European invasion.

As the Inca empire expanded through the conquests and alliances undertaken by successive kings, the Incas came into contact with rich and vibrant traditions of the origins of noble families and dynasties – as in Lambayeque and Moche – in far flung corners of the empire. The challenge that confronted the Incas in each such instance was not only to incorporate those provincial mythic-histories into imperial traditions but to do so in ways

Moche spouted vessel in the form of a balsa raft with two occupants.

that preserved the sanctity and the centrality of the Inca dynasty. This was the principal task – that is, the continual reworking of local and regional origin myths – that confronted the amautas and quipucamayoqs who were responsible for preserving and reconciling the mythic-histories of Tahuantinsuyu. In the particular case at hand, that of the relationship between the Incas and the lords of Chimor, we have several accounts of how this (or a similar) encounter was considered to have proceeded from the Inca point of view. One such account is in the work of Garcilaso de la Vega, who gives the following account of how the Incas told the story of what happened when the Inca Tupac Yupanqui marched against the once mighty lord Chimu:

'The brave Chimu, his arrogance and pride now tamed, appeared before the prince with as much submission and humility, and grovelled on the ground before him, worshipping him and repeating the same request [for pardon] as he had made through his ambassadors. The prince received him affectionately in order to relieve the grief he was evincing. He bade two of the captains raise him from the ground, and after hearing him, told him that all that was past was forgiven . . . The Inca had not come to deprive him of his estates and authority, but to improve his idolatrous religion, his laws and customs.'

Myths of the Hatunruna (the commoners)

We turn now from the mythologies of peoples of pre-Inca states on the north coast to explore mythic traditions retained by commoner populations in the Inca empire. As was true in the case of the collection and recording of myths in Cusco and on the north coast of Peru, so in the provinces do our sources consist of accounts written down after the Spanish conquest. However, the provincial documentation recounting myths and portraying various aspects of the religious beliefs and practices of people in the countryside tends to be both later and less voluminous than that relating to the same subject matter in Cusco.

Many of the accounts detailing provincial mythologies come to us by way of information collected by local priests during the early seventeenth century who went out into the countryside to root out what the Spaniards referred to as 'idolatries'. This referred to the worship of ancestral mummies, celestial bodies and a vast array of notable features of the landscape, such as mountain peaks, springs and caves. Later, we will examine information from a couple of documents that derives from priests' reports from a few such investigations in the central and northern Peruvian Andes. We will turn first, however, to a remarkable document from the seventeenth century that was drawn up with a similar objective in mind – the discovery of idolatrous beliefs and practices – but which contains one of the most complete and coherent accounts available to us of provincial mythology.

The gods and men of Huarochirí

The document we are concerned with now is commonly referred to as the 'Huarochirí Manuscript'. The province of Huarochirí is located to the east of present-day Lima, in the westernmost chain of mountains in central Peru. The manuscript, written in the Quechua language, dates from around 1608. We do not know who actually wrote the material down (it is likely that it was written by a native), although we do know that its collection and recording were carried out under the direction of a local 'extirpator of idolatries', Francisco de Avila. In order to appreciate the events and actions recorded in this remarkable document, it is helpful to give a general overview of the social and political milieu within which it was produced.

The inhabitants of the region of Huarochirí were predominantly members of ayllus of the Yauyos ethnic and cultural group. The Yauyos ayllus were divided into two parts: *Anan* ('upper') *Yauyos*, and *Lurin* ('lower') *Yauyos*. The information recorded in the manuscript is written from the point of view of a couple of subgroups – the Checa and Concha – of Lower Yauyos. As a general classificatory label of a certain type of people, the 'Yauyos' were considered to be late arrivals to this region, pastoralists who came into the area, perhaps from the south. The invading Yauyos pastoralists established themselves in the Huarochirí area in opposition to the autochthonous population of lowland agriculturalists. In fact, however, it seems likely that the aboriginal farmers of the area were themselves of Yauyos origin. That is, the agriculturalists had moved into this area in remote antiquity, became assimilated, and were then overrun by this later migration of peoples of the same Yauyos ancestry.

Huallallo Carhuincho was the principal deity worshipped by the aboriginal peoples of Yauyos. Huallallo was a fearsome, fire-breathing volcanic deity who was given to the practice of cannibalism. For instance, he commanded that every household in Lower Yauyos should have only two children, and that one of the children was to be given to him to eat. In those primordial times, when Huallallo ruled unchallenged, the climate of the highlands was comparable to the coastal lowlands (the *Yungas*); that is, like the Yungas, the area of Huarochirí in those days was warm, and the land was filled with huge snakes, toucans (a kind of tropical bird), and all kinds of animals associated in later times with the coast. The principal deity of the recent Yauyos invaders was Pariacaca. In the Huarochirí Manuscript, 'Pariacaca', which was the name of a high mountain peak, is portrayed as a huaca (sacred object, or place) who moves about the countryside in the personification of a culture hero, or patron deity.

The mythological accounting of the origins of the world as told in Huarochirí begins after Huallallo Carhuincho had held dominion for some time. The huaca Pariacaca was then born on a mountain top in the form of five eggs that became five falcons that were transformed into five men. These men were believed by the author(s) of the Huarochirí Manuscript to have been the ancestors of the principal families and ritual groups of the recent Yauyos pastoralists who lived thereabouts. The powerful mountain deity, or huaca, Pariacaca challenged Huallallo Carhuincho for supremacy in this area. Pariacaca prophesied that he would fight Huallallo Carhuincho and drive him away. Pariacaca said that he would would fight with water, whereas Huallallo vowed to fight with fire. Their struggle is described in the document as follows:

'Pariacaca, since he was five persons, began to rain down from five directions. That rain was yellow and red rain. Then, flashing as lightning, he blazed out from five directions. From early in the morning to the setting of the sun, Huallallo Carhuincho flamed up in the form of a giant fire reaching almost to the heavens, never letting himself be extinguished. And the waters, the rains of Pariacaca, rushed down toward Ura Cocha, the lower lake. Since it wouldn't have fit in, one of Pariacaca's five selves, the one called Llacsa Churapa, knocked down a mountain and dammed the waters from below. Once he impounded these waters they formed a lake . . . As the waters filled the lake they almost submerged that burning fire. And Pariacaca kept flashing lightning bolts at him, never letting him rest. Finally Huallallo Carhuincho fled toward the low country, the Antis [Antisuyu].'

Pariacaca next fought against a female huaca, a demon named Mana Ñamca, who was an ally of Huallallo Carhuincho. Pariacaca defeated this woman as well, driving her into the ocean, to the west. Pariacaca then set about establishing his own cult. These struggles were the defining set of events in the displacement of the autochthonous agriculturalist population and their deity, Huallallo Carhuincho, by the invading Yauyos pastoralists, the latter of whom were the chief adherents of the cult of Pariacaca.

The Huarochirí Manuscript also attests to the presence of a deity named 'Viracocha', the same name as borne by the creator deity whom we encountered in the origin myth from Lake Titicaca. The compilers of the Huarochirí document claimed not to know whether or not this Viracocha, who was known as Coniraya Viracocha, lived before or after the time of Huallallo Carhuincho. Whenever it was, Coniraya Viracocha was a creator deity. He made the villages in the region, and by his words alone he brought the agricultural fields and terraces into existence. He also created the irrigation canals, an act which he accomplished by tossing down the flower of a type of reed, called *pupuna*, to form the channels.

Coniraya Viracocha went around as a wandering, friendless beggar, dressed in ripped and tattered clothing. People who did not recognize him shouted insults at him. At this time, there was a beautiful female huaca in the area named Cavillaca. She was a virgin, and Coniraya decided that he desperately wanted to sleep with her; however, the beautiful Cavillaca would have nothing to do with him. One day, Cavillaca was weaving beneath a *lúcuma* tree. This is a type of evergreen tree common on the coast, which bears fruit with a yellowish-orange pulp. Coniraya Viracocha transformed himself into a bird and flew into the lúcuma tree. He put his semen into a ripened fruit and dropped it beside Cavillaca. The woman ate the fruit happily, and she became pregnant. Nine months later, Cavillaca gave birth to a boy, still not knowing who had fathered him.

When the boy was one year old, Cavillaca determined to find out who had impregnated her. Thus she called together all the *vilcas* and *huacas* – the powerful male deities, mountains and other sacred places. The vilcas and huacas all came dressed in their finest clothing, each one excitedly saying, 'It's me! It's me she'll love!' Coniraya Viracocha came as well, but he arrived still dressed in tattered clothing. When the vilcas and huacas had all seated themselves, Cavillaca asked which one of them was the father of her child. When no one spoke up, Cavillaca put the boy on the ground, saying that he would crawl to his father. The child crawled along the line of seated vilcas and huacas until he came to Coniraya Viracocha. The boy brightened up and climbed into his father's lap.

Cavillaca became furious at this turn of events; how could she have given birth to the child of such a beggar as this? Enraged, she snatched up the child and headed straight for the ocean. She went out into the sea, near the site of Pachacamac, a great pilgrimage centre and oracle on the central coast (just to the south of present-day Lima). There, Cavillaca and her son were transformed into stone. They can still be seen off the coast today, near the ruins of Pachacamac. Coniraya Viracocha was distressed at this turn of events and determined to go in search of them. He sped off toward the coast, asking all whom he encountered along the way if they had seen Cavillaca pass by.

As it turns out, Coniraya encountered a series of animals and birds on his journey: a condor, skunk, puma, fox, falcon, and parakeets. He asked each one in turn about Cavillaca. Depending on the answer they gave him – that is, whether they gave him good or bad news – he assigned to them good or bad traits and fortune. For instance, when he asked the condor about Cavillaca, the bird said that she was nearby and that Coniraya would surely find her soon. Coniraya told the condor he would live a long life, would always have plenty of food, eating dead animals from the mountain slopes, and that if anyone should kill him (the condor), that person would die as well. However, when Coniraya asked the skunk if he had seen Cavillaca, the skunk said he would never find her, that she had gone far away. Thus Coniraya said to the skunk that he would never go around in the daytime; rather, he would always go out at night, stinking, and people would be disgusted by him. In this way, Coniraya Viracocha performed the creative task of naming the animals and giving them their habits and characteristics just as the myths centring on Lake Titicaca tell us Conticci Viracocha did in his own journey of creation from the mountains to the Ecuadorian coast.

When Coniraya reached the seashore, he went to the site of Pachacamac. There, he came upon the place where Pachacamac's two daughters were guarded by a snake. The girls' mother, Urpay Huachac, was away at the time. Coniraya seduced the elder sister, and then tried to do the same with the younger. Before he could succeed, however, the girl turned into a dove and flew away. Now, at that time there were no fish in the ocean. The only ones that existed were bred by Urpay Huachac, who kept them in a small pond near the site of Pachacamac. In his rage, Coniraya Viracocha scattered the fish in the ocean and since then the sea has been filled with fish.

A pyramid compound at Pachacamac, with Inca temple of the sun in the background.

Coniraya Viracocha never succeeded in finding Cavillaca and her son. Instead, the Huarochirí Manuscript says, he travelled along the coast 'for a long, long time, tricking lots of local huacas and people, too'. It is particularly notable that the exploits of Coniraya Viracocha on the coast are recounted in the Huarochirí Manuscript by people who lived in the high Andes. This mythological link between the two worlds, coast and highlands, prompts us to recognize the intimate relationship between the different but closely related peoples and resources of these two regions. We should explore this relationship more directly.

Viracocha and Pachacamac

Part of the task of mythology in pre-Columbian and continuing into early colonial times was to explore and explain the distinctions and linkages between the two worlds of the coast and the highlands. One of the ways this exploration is reflected in the myths is in terms of the identities of creator deities, such as Viracocha and Pachacamac. These two are seen in the myths in a way like face-to-face revolving mirrors: at one moment they are distinct and separate, while at the next moment they appear to be identical. In fact, the question of the relationship between Viracocha and Pachacamac is further complicated in the Huarochirí Manuscript because the people in this area – midway between the Incas in the south central highlands, on one side, and the Yungas and other peoples of the coast, on the other side – often substituted the highland/coastal opposition between Viracocha and Pachacamac respectively with that between the Sun and Pachacamac. That is, the document cites the Huarochirí view to the effect that: 'In the highlands, they say, the Incas worshipped the sun as the object of their adoration from Titicaca, saying, "It is he who made us Inca!" From the lowlands, they worshipped Pachacamac, saying, "It is he who made us Inca!"'

According to one of the interpreters of the Huarochirí document (Salomon), this manuscript links, at the same time as it juxtaposes, the creator of the highlands (the Sun) with that of the coast (Pachacamac). What is elided in this relationship – although it is evoked in the above reference to 'Titicaca' – is the highland creator deity, Viracocha Pachayachiachic. These seemingly contradictory references to different, yet apparently complementary, creator deities have been the cause of an enormous amount of confusion from the colonial period to the present day. In general, it seems that the creator was identified by different names in various parts of the empire, while retaining a similar, core set of characteristics and performing similar creative works from one place to the next. The latter include dressing as a beggar and punishing those who offend him while he is in this state, naming and assigning typical traits to animals and birds of the realm, and the creation, destruction and recreation of humanity. For the moment, we should turn our attention to Pachacamac, for we have not yet explored the characteristics of this manifestation of the Andean creator deity in any detail.

As mentioned earlier, the name 'Pachacamac' referred among other things to a pilgrimage site on the central coast of Peru, a few kilometres south of Lima. The site was probably recognized as an important oracle as early as the Middle Horizon and was, until the incorporation of the site into the Inca empire, probably known as *Irma*, or *Illma*. When the Incas conquered the central coast, they took possession of the site but retained it as an oracle and a pilgrimage site. In addition, they built a large Temple of the Sun there, installing alongside the ancient oracle a cult with priests dedicated to the Inca (highland) solar deity.

Antonio de la Calancha left us one of the principal myths concerning the deity Pachacamac, a myth in which the Sun and Pachacamac are in intimate association with each other. In fact, Pachacamac is introduced in this myth as the 'son of the Sun', thus placing the coastal deity in a subordinate position vis á vis the highland deity. The myth goes as follows (as summarized in a work by Franklin Pease, see Further Reading).

At the beginning of time, Pachacamac created a human couple, the first man and woman. However, there was no food for them and the man soon died. The woman begged the Sun for help, whereupon he impregnated her with his rays. The woman gave birth to a boy after only four days. Pachacamac was jealous and angry at this turn of events, and he killed the boy and tore him into pieces. Pachacamac then used the dismembered body to provide for the want of food in the land. That is, he sowed the teeth of the corpse, and from them corn sprang up. He planted the ribs and bones, and yucca (manioc) tubers sprouted from them. The flesh was planted and it gave forth vegetables, such as cucumbers, and fruiting trees.

The Sun then took the penis and navel of the corpse and created another son for himself; this child was named *Vichama*, or *Villama*. Like his father, the Sun, Vichama wanted to travel so he set off on a journey. When Vichama departed, Pachacamac killed the woman, the same one whom he had earlier created. This woman was, in fact, Vichama's mother as Vichama was made – by a kind of 'cloning' process – of the penis and navel of the woman's first son. Pachacamac fed the remains of the woman to the vultures and condors.

Pachacamac then created a new human couple, who began to repopulate the land; he also named authorities (curacas) to rule over the people. When Vichama returned from his journey, he reassembled his mother and brought her back to life. Out of fear of reprisal for having killed Vichama's mother, Pachacamac fled to the ocean, sinking into the sea in front of the temple of Vichama/Pachacamac. Vichama turned the people whom Pachacamac had recently created into stone. He later repented of his deed and transformed the stones which had previously been curacas into huacas.

Vichama now asked his father, the Sun, to create a new race of humanity. The sun sent three eggs, of gold, silver and copper. The golden egg was the origin of the curacas and nobles; the silver egg gave rise to women; and from the copper egg came the commoners and their families. Elsewhere along the central and south coast, Calancha reports, it was believed that Pachacamac sent four stars to the earth. Two of the stars were male and two were female. From the first set were generated the kings and nobility, and from the second came the commoners.

The joining of Pachacamac and the Sun in this myth may well represent another example of the process alluded to earlier of the reworking of local myths to reflect a highland, Inca perspective. In this instance, the Sun represented the surrogate for the Incas. What we do not know, of course, is to what degree peoples of the central coast around the powerful oracle of Pachacamac might have actually bought into – that is, retold voluntarily – this imperial reworking of the local origin myth.

As noted earlier, the myth of Pachacamac and the Sun recounted above is recorded by Antonio de la Calancha in a chronicle written in 1638. At about this same time, a momentous process of investigating native idolatries in the highlands to the east of the site of Pachacamac was well under way.

Idolatry and the persistence of pre-Columbian beliefs and practices

The proselytizing of native Andean peoples carried out by various orders of the Catholic clergy began during the earliest days of the conquest, in the 1530s and 1540s, and was both intense and continuous. Nonetheless, by the end of the sixteenth century and into the early seventeenth century, as the clergy moved into remoter regions of the Andes, it became increasingly clear to them that the native peoples in these scattered mountainous settlements were continuing the worship of mountains, 'pagan' creator deities, and ancestral mummies, as well as the sun, moon and stars.

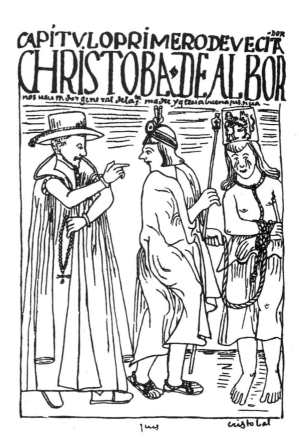

CAPITVLOPRIMERODEVECĩᵈᵒʳ
CHRISTOBA·DE·ALBOR
nos uen m Jor gen ral dela q̃ madre yq̃ ecia buena jusㅋ῀a

The priest Cristobal de Albornoz
(left) directing the capture of an
accused idolater.

This discovery greatly concerned the Spanish priests, for it suggested to them that while the armies of Spain had long ago won the battle against the Inca armies, they might be steadily losing the war against the native deities. More drastic and concerted efforts were required in order to root out and exterminate the worship of native idols, 'witches' and spirits. Therefore a number of vigorous campaigns against idolatrous practices were launched between 1610 and 1690, in the course of which the Catholic priests, relying on the support of the local lords (curacas), systematically questioned native peoples about the objects or deities they worshipped, their methods of curing diseases and divining the future, and other 'heretical' beliefs and practices. The records drawn up from these campaigns, only a handful of which have so far been published, are known as *idolatrías*.

The documents produced by the idolatries campaigns represent an unparalleled source of information on many aspects of everyday life, including religious beliefs and practices, in Andean communities at this time. In addition, they provide a background and a foundation for contextualizing and interpreting the great cosmic myths and the myths of the Inca state as the latter were recorded in the earlier 'official' documents and chronicles – based on Spanish inquiries among noble informants – of the Inca past.

The Idolatries

The most illuminating aspect of the idolatry records after almost four centuries is the intimate connection they illustrate between the people living in a community and the host of sacred objects and spiritual entities occupying the landscape around them. One particularly detailed and poignant set of accounts comes from the highlands of central Peru, around the town of Cajatambo. The people in this area, like those in many other parts of the Andes during this period, were divided into numerous ayllus. In Cajatambo, the ayllus were grouped together according to the two different 'types' of people that were considered to inhabit this land: the Guari and the Llacuaz. We will see that the characteristics of, and the relations between, these two types of people were similar to what we saw earlier in the case of the agriculturalists and pastoralists of the region of Huarochirí.

The Guari of Cajatambo were aboriginal lowland or valley-dwelling peoples who had founded the existing towns in the region. The patron deity of the Guaris was a giant god, associated with caves, who is identified in the literature as 'Huari'. These people also worshipped the night-time sun – that is, the sun when it passed through the underworld, moving along its watery passage from sundown to sunrise. It was said that the ancestors of the Guari peoples had come into this area in remote times either from the ocean, to the west, or from Lake Titicaca. The Guaris were primarily corn-cultivators who worshipped sacred amulets, called *canopas*, which were considered to control the fertility of the maize fields.

The other side of the great social divide in the region of Cajatambo was composed of the Llacuaz peoples. These were puna or highland dwelling people whose economy was based on potato cultivation and the herding of llamas and alpacas. The principal deity of the Llacuaz peoples was 'Llibiac', who was primarily a thunder-and-lightning god. The Llacuaz also worshipped the sun of the daytime – the sun as it passed overhead from sunrise to sunset – and the stars. The Llacuaz were considered to be late arrivals to this area, migrants who had come into the territory at some time in the not-too-distant past and had conquered the Guari.

The ritual life in the settlements of Cajatambo commemorated the Llacuaz conquest of the Guari, as well as the subsequent founding of a confederation between the two groups. Each side of this two-part (moiety) confederation adopted certain rituals and ceremonies of the opposing half. That is, rituals were celebrated in a reciprocal fashion: the Guaris celebrated rituals on behalf of the Llacuazs, and vice versa. The two groups also celebrated some rituals and festivals jointly, and they also jointly revered certain sacred objects, as well as numerous places in the landscape that were identified as the burial places of sacrificial victims, the capacochas. These sacrificial victims established links between the local people and the Incas, the latter of whom had been considered by the Guaris and Llacuazs to have been the owners of the entire land.

The various ayllus of Guaris and Llacuazes each had special links to huacas in the surrounding countryside, such as mountain peaks, springs and caves. The huacas were thought to exert influence over the life and destiny of the particular group of people who worshipped them. The most powerful huacas were the high mountains, each of which had its own name, spirit (or spirits), and a particular kinship relationship to other mountains in the region. In addition, any especially large or prominent boulders, called *huancas*, were considered sacred and were believed to represent, or contain the essence of, an ancestor of one or more of the local ayllus.

The mythological traditions of ayllus within the region of Cajatambo were composed largely of stories recounting how the spiritual essences of ayllu ancestors had come to be lodged within the surrounding mountains, rocky outcrops, and other prominent features of the landscape. Stories also told how these sacred places and entities had interacted with each other in the distant past. Another geographical feature that was of great ritual and mythological significance for the peoples of Cajatambo were the many caves, called *machay*, that dotted the mountainsides. As we saw earlier, caves held a place of particular importance in Inca myths about the origin of the first king of the empire. In Cajatambo, caves were the places of origin of the ancestors of the Guari and Llacuaz ayllus, as well as the repositories of the mummies (*malquis*) of deceased ayllu members.

The numbers of ancestral mummies stored in these caves were truly astonishing. For instance, one idolatry account from 1656–8 lists the following numbers of ancestral mummies found in caves, or in abandoned towns around the settlement of San Pedro de Hacas: in Yanaqui, 214 bodies; in Quirca, 471 bodies; in Ayllu Carampa, 738 bodies; and in Ayllu Picoca, 402 bodies! These collections of malquis were worshipped by the living inhabitants of their respective towns. The mummies were dressed in new clothing at certain times of the year, and offerings of food and drink were made to them at planting and harvesting seasons.

The information recorded in the idolatry accounts thus reveals, even a century or two after the Spanish conquest, how people in the Andean countryside viewed the past and the present, the living and the dead, and the land and the people who lived on it as interconnected, continuous and fully complementary. The complementary oppositions between lowlanders and highlanders, autochthonous peoples and migrants, conquerors and conquered, corn (maize) and potato cultivators (and pastoralists), sun and moon and other such divisions that appear in the beliefs of peoples in Cajatambo in the seventeenth century were entirely consistent with similar beliefs described in the earliest chronicles of the Inca empire.

These beliefs, which formed the religious and ideological foundations of myths detailing the nature of relations among ayllus and ethnic groups in the empire, continued to inform the mythological traditions of Andean peoples during much of the colonial era. But beyond a similarity between pre-Hispanic and colonial beliefs and myths, there were also traditions linking the two eras; these were – and still are – recounted in villages throughout the Andes in myths such as those narrating the death, and predicting the rebirth, of the Inca.

The Inca past in the Andean present

Ethnographic studies in Andean communities did not begin in earnest until after the end of World War II. By the end of the 1950s, a number of anthropologists had assembled a corpus of myths and legends from Quechua- and Aymara-speaking communities throughout the Andes. There are two mythic traditions to point to in particular as they will allow us to reflect broadly on the long-term importance of the image and persona of the Inca, as well as the uses to which myths have been put, in the Andean world. One of these traditions concerns a body of myths relating to what we may term the theme of the 'dying and reviving Inca'. Such myths, shared as they are by communities throughout the Andes, represent a source of pan-Andean unity, somewhat in the manner of the cosmic myths with Lake Titicaca as the place of origin that were told in Inca times. The other type of myth that we should look at briefly here concerns the linkage between a local myth of origin and its connection to local and state validation. Interestingly enough, we may again turn in this regard to the uses of myths of origin in the town of Pacaritambo, the origin place of the first Inca, Manco Capac.

The dying and reviving Inca

Many myths about the Incas that are shared broadly throughout the Andes today revolve around the millenarian theme of the return of the Inca. The central character in these myths is *Inkarrí*, a name based on a combination of the terms Inca and the Spanish *rey* ('king').

The myth of Inkarrí is millenarian in the sense that it foretells a time in the future when the Andean world will undergo a cataclysmic transformation involving the destruction of the Spanish-dominated world, which has been in place since the European invasion in the seventeenth century, and the reinstatement of the Inca as supreme ruler. The millenarian overtones here are perfectly in tune with the age-old Andean notion of 'pachacuti', the revolution, or reversal of time and space. A number of versions of the Inkarrí myth were collected in the 1950s by the great Peruvian anthropologist José María Arguedas in the southern Peruvian town of Puquio. One version of this myth goes as follows.

'They say Inkarrí was the son of a woman who was a savage. His father, they say, was Father Sun. That savage woman bore Inkarrí; Father Sun begat Inkarrí.

The Inca king had three women. The work of the Inca is on Ak'nu. On K'ellk'ata Plain the wine, the *chicha* [corn beer] and the *aguar-diente* [cane alchohol] are boiling.

Inkarrí drove the stones with a whip, ordering them about. Afterwards, he founded a city. K'ellk'ata could have been Cusco, so they say.

. . . Inkarrí confined the wind. . . [and] he bound Father Sun, so time would last, so the day would last, so that Inkarrí would be able to do what he had to do.

When he had bound the wind to the mountain [of Osk'onta], he hurled a golden rod from the top of Big Osk'onta, saying, "Will Cusco fit?" It did not fit into K'ellk'ata Plain. He threw the rod far down, saying "It does not fit in." Cusco was moved to where it is. How far off might that be? We of the living generation do not know. The old generation, before Atahualpa, knew that.

The Spanish Inca imprisoned Inkarrí, his equal. Where, we do not know. The head is all that's left of Inkarrí, they say. From the head he's growing inward; toward the feet he's growing, they say.

He will return then, Inkarrí, when his body is whole. He has not returned until now. He is to return to us, if God sees fit. But we do not know, they say, if God is to decide that he should return.'

The decapitation of Atahualpa.

The origins of the myth of Inkarrí as recounted in Puquio and in countless other cities, towns and villages in the Andes seem to go back to events that occurred during the forty years or so immediately following the Spanish conquest. One event was the decapitation of the last Inca ruler, Atahualpa, by Francisco Pizarro soon after the defeat of the Inca armies in Cajamarca. The other major, traumatic event was another decapitation of a native leader by the Spanish authorities – the victim in this case was Tupac Amaru, who led a revolt against the Spanish in the 1560s and 1570s. Tupac Amaru was beheaded in the plaza of Cusco, by order of Franciso de Toledo, in 1572.

In both these instances of the decapitation of an Inca – or, in the second case, a 'neo-Inca' – the story apparently spread throughout the countryside that the head had been spirited away and buried. In some accounts, the head was taken to Lima; in others, it was taken to Cusco. In either case, once the head was placed in the ground, it is believed to have begun to regrow the body. When the body is complete, the Inca will return, and the world will undergo a pachacuti.

Living at, and using, the Inca place of origin

The town of Pacaritambo, site of the cave of Tambo Toco, traditional birthplace of the Inca Manco Capac and his siblings, lies some 26 km due south of the old Inca capital of Cusco. Having myself lived in this town during more than two years of ethnographic fieldwork in the 1980s, I can attest to the extraordinary interest and pride on the part of local people in the position this village occupies in Peruvian history. People continually point out places in the landscape – a rock outcrop with what appear to be the footprints of a llama impressed in the stone, a depression in a boulder, or a split mountain peak – that are believed to be the visible markings of the passing of the Incas at the beginning of time. A kilometre or so from the town is a small cave, which local residents identify as the site of Tambo Toco. Thus the landscape around the town and cave is a living remnant of the Inca origin myth.

In fact, the status of Pacaritambo as the origin place of the Incas is reinforced today by the government-issue primary school textbooks, used throughout Peru, which recount a truncated, child's version of the origin myth. This officially sanctioned version of the origin myth is a source of considerable pride for the people of the town, but in addition to the local importance of the continuing identification of Pacaritambo as the origin place of the first Inca, this tradition has on occasion been used by outsiders in some rather novel ways. Perhaps the most striking such instance involved a past president of Peru, Fernando Belaúnde Terry.

Upon first entering office in 1964 Belaúnde Terry visited Pacaritambo in a move that was blatantly intended to incorporate into the foundations of his presidency the legitimacy afforded by contact with the origin place of the first Inca king. The president took a helicopter from Cusco, landing in the plaza in the middle of the town of Pacaritambo. There, he received a traditional wooden staff of office, called a *vara*, shook the hands of local officials,

The cave recognized today as Tambo Toco.

and then helicoptered back to Cusco, whence he returned to the presidential palace in Lima. Today, people who were in the plaza then, and who perhaps shook the president's hand, tell the story of his (literal) whirlwind visit, exaggerating various elements of the story for the benefit of their companions.

Whatever the true character of the Incas in their own day, therefore, and whether or not the head of the last Inca is regrowing its body in the present day, the memory and image of the Incas continue to hold tremendous power and meaning for the people who live in the land that was once Tahuantinsuyu.

Suggestions for further reading

There are a number of recently published books in English that provide good, general overviews of Andean archaeology up to, and including, the Inca empire. These include: Michael E. Moseley, *The Incas and Their Ancestors* (London, 1992); Adriana von Hagen and Craig Morris, *The Cities of the Ancient Andes* (London, 1998); and Jonathan Haas, Sheila Pozorski and Thomas Pozorski (eds), *The Origins and Development of the Andean State* (Cambridge, 1987). Other archaeological studies concerning developments in the Andes leading up to the Incas include: Richard Burger, *Chavín and the Origins of Andean Civilization* (London, 1992); Alan Kolata, *Tiwanaku: Portrait of an Andean Civilization* (Oxford and Cambridge MA, 1993); Katharina J. Schreiber, *Wari Imperialism in Middle Horizon Peru* (Ann Arbor, 1992); and William H. Isbell, *Mummies and Mortuary Monuments* (Austin, 1997).

For archaeological and ethnohistorical studies dealing specifically with the Incas, see Brian S. Bauer, *The Development of the Inca State* (Austin, 1992) and Martti Pärssinen, *Tawantinsuyu: The Inca State and Its Political Organization* (Helsinki, 1992). Still one of the best overviews of Inca culture in late pre-Hispanic times is John H. Rowe, 'Inca culture at the time of the Spanish conquest', in Julian H. Steward (ed.), *Handbook of South American Indians*, Vol. 2, Bulletin #143: 183–330 (Washington, DC, 1946). For a work documenting the relationship between state and ayllu in Andean economic organization, see John V. Murra, *The Economic Organization of the Inca State* (Greenwich CT, 1980). The standard source for studying the social, ritual and political organization of Inca Cusco is R.Tom Zuidema, *The Ceque System of Cuzco: The Social Organization of the Capital of the Inca* (Leiden, 1964).

There have been few good, English-language overviews of the Spanish chroniclers who wrote on Inca myth and history. One of the most authoritative and comprehensive of such works in Spanish is Raúl Porras Barrenechea's *Los cronistas del Perú* (1528–1650) (Lima, 1986). For a set of studies on the native Andean chroniclers, see Rolena Adorno (ed.), *From Oral to Written Expression: Native Andean Chronicles of the Early Colonial Period* (Syracuse, 1982). The reader is also referred to the collection of translated passages from various chroniclers' accounts of Inca myths in Harold Osborne's *South American Mythology* (London, 1968). The best study to date discussing the intellectual and theological backgrounds of many of the chroniclers in relation to their accounts of Inca mythic-histories is Sabine MacCormack's *Religion in the Andes: Vision and Imagination in Early Colonial Peru* (Princeton NJ, 1991).

For works concerning the cosmic myths of origin focusing on Lake Titicaca and Tiahuanaco, see Verónica Salles-Reese, *From Viracocha to the Virgin of Copacabana: Representation of the Sacred at Lake Titicaca* (Austin, 1997); Thérèse Bouysse-Cassagne, *Lluvias y Cenizas: Dos Pachacuti en la Historia* (La Paz, 1988); and Franklin Pease, *El Dios Creador Andino* (Lima, 1973).

For a study specifically dealing with the role of colonial-period residents of the town of Pacaritambo in recounting Inca myths of origin beginning at their home community, see Gary Urton, *The History of a Myth: Pacariqtambo and the Origin of the Inkas* (Austin, 1990). For a general study of the Inca origin myths and their relation to the political organization of the capital city, see R. Tom Zuidema, *Inca Civilization in Cuzco* (Austin, 1990). A good, highly readable account of the Spanish conquest of the Incas that pays special attention to the early colonial history of the Cusco region is John Hemming's *The Conquest of the Incas* (New York and London, 1970).

For an excellent collection of articles dealing with the mythic-histories and archaeological records of the Chimu and other Peruvian north coastal societies, see María Rostworowski de Diez Canseco and Michael E. Moseley (eds), *The Northern Dynasties: Kingship and Statecraft in Chimor* (Washington DC, 1990). On this same topic, see María Rostworowski, *Costa peruana prehispanica* (Lima, 1989). For an excellent overview of the cultural context for reading the Huarochirí Manuscript, as well as a definitive transcription and English translation of the Quechua text itself, see Frank Salomon and George L. Urioste, *The Huarochirí Manuscript* (Austin, 1991). Kenneth Mills' *Idolatry and Its Enemies: Colonial Andean Religion and Extirpation, 1640-1750* (Princeton NJ, 1997) is an excellent study of the idolatrías process and reports. In addition, many of the documents deriving from the idolatry investigations and trials in the region of Cajatambo have been collected in Pierre Duviols' *Cultura Andina y Repression: Procesos y visitas de idolatrías y hechicerías Cajatambo, Siglo XVII* (Cusco, 1986).

Accounts of a few versions of myths of Incarrí are to be found in the short ethnography of Puquio published with José María Arguedas novel, *Yawar Fiesta* (Austin, 1985). For an excellent study of the Incarrí myths, see Mercedes López-Baralt, *El Retorno del Inca Rey: Mito y profecía en el mundo andino* (Fuenlabrada, 1987). On the theme of utopianism and millenarian ideology in contemporary Peru, see Alberto Flores Galindo, *Buscando un Inca: Identidad y Utopia en los Andes* (Havana, 1985).

Picture credits

Index